from *Dubai,* with *love*

Samaira Pareek

First Published in March 2023

ISBN: 978-93-5741-361-9

BLUEROSE PUBLISHERS

www.BlueRoseONE.com
info@bluerosepublishers.com
+91 8882 898 898

Cover Design:
Samaira Pareek

Typographic Design:
Pooja Sharma

Distributed by: BlueRose, Amazon, Flipkart

Playlist - English

This is what heartbreak feels like - JVKE

Moral of the Story - Ashe

Flowers - Lauren Spencer Smith

GROWING UP IS _____ - Ruel

Ceilings - Lizzy McAlpine

Consume - Chase Atlantic

Fantasy - Bazzi

Friends - Chase Atlantic

Shameless - Camila Cabello

This is what falling in love feels like - JVKE

Teenage Dream - Stephen Dawes

Golden hour - JVKE

I Like Me Better - Lauv

Playlist - Desi

Insane - AP Dhillon, Shinda Kahlon, Gurinder Gill, Gminxr

Excuses - AP Dhillon, Gurinder Gill, Intense

Sanam Re - Mithoon, Arijit Singh

Pasoori - Shae Gill, Ali Sethi

Kesariya - Pritam, Arijit Singh, Amitabh Bhattacharya

Dil Diyan Gallan - Vishal-Shekhar, Julius Packiam, Atif Aslam, Irshad Kamil

Lover - Diljit Dosanjh

Janam Janam - Pritam, Arijit Singh, Antara Mitra

Zaalima - Harshdeep Kaur, Arijit Singh

Maula Mere Maula - Roop Kumar Rathod

Tum Hi Ho - Arijit Singh

Dil Ko Karaar Aaya - Yasser Desai, Neha Kakkar, Rajat Nagpal

Contents

Kintsugi

noun

I. a traditional Japanese pottery repair technique in which lacquer mixed with precious metals, especially gold, is used to fill cracks and replace missing pieces.

Chapter 1
Kiara

"Kiara? Earth to Kiara? Hello? Anybody in there?"

I woke up to find Jai standing over my bed, fully dressed and trying to wake me up. "Mmmm, five more minutes."

"Yeah, if you want to miss Amara's wedding then sure, five more minutes sounds fine."

"What?!" I turned around to peer at the alarm clock next to my bed, the screen flashed '08:45' angrily in large red letters. Who knew an alarm clock could be so condescending. I practically flew out of bed and panicked my way through brushing my teeth and putting on some half-decent clothes. I say half-decent because I was still wearing my polka dot pyjamas with an 'I love AP Dhillon' t-shirt. Not exactly designer stuff.

"Why didn't you wake me sooner?"

"I've been trying to wake you up for thirty minutes. Even an entire construction team in your room wouldn't wake you."

I bolted from the car and ran into the house, hunting for my cousin.

"There she is, our sleeping beauty."

"Yes, here, and definitely not late or half asleep still." Everyone in the room laughed. I might be the CFO of a multi-billion dollar company and have a fiancé, but I'm essentially still a baby in everyone else's eyes. Although my sleeping habits don't exactly work in my favour.

I got my hair and makeup done and went downstairs to find Jai.

"Wow, you look…incredible."

I did a small twirl and tried not to blush. Even after four years, he still makes the inside of my cheeks heat with one look.

"You look pretty damn good yourself," he mock bowed and pulled me into his arms, kissing the top of my head.

I looked around the room, "This is going to be us in a year," I whispered into his ear. He smiled down at me, but it didn't quite reach his eyes.

"You okay?"

He's probably just tired. Don't overthink this.

"Yeah, I'm fine. Shall we?"

I smiled and nodded. We made our way onto the beach for the Mehendi where everyone was starting to gather. The dhols played in one corner, while the DJ blasted music in the other. The entire beach looked like a sandy flower field as far as the eye could see. Nothing but the best for Amara and Nick. I wandered off to find my friends and make the usual rounds.

I didn't make it very far before Pinky Auntie caught up with me, "Kiara, beta, hello!" She sashayed over in her bright pink sari, her kitten heels making small clicking sounds as she walked. Pinky Auntie was one of the more obnoxious Aunties, and it always served well to steer clear of her.

"Hi Pinky Auntie, how are you?"

Let's just get this over with quickly, Kiara. Painlessly. As quick and painless as possible.

"I'm well beta, very well. So, tell me, how are things?"

"Good Auntie, very good. I was actually just appointed CFO of the company."

"Ah good, good," I knew exactly what Pinky Auntie was getting ready to ask about, especially with the way she was rushing through the conversation about my career, "So I hear you're getting married next year, congratulations. That Jai of yours is quite a catch."

I was tempted to avoid the marriage subject entirely and torture her with more talk about my job but that wouldn't exactly go in my favor, it quintessentially meant more screentime with Pinky Auntie. Definitely not quick. Definitely not painless.

I looked over to where my fiancé was talking to Nick and his friends and I couldn't help but blush a little, "Yes, he is."

She smiled and opened her mouth to say something that—based on the somewhat evil expression on her face—

didn't look like it was going to be very pleasant, before a pair of arms grabbed me around my waist.

"Can I steal her from you, Auntie?"

Pinky Auntie smiled a somewhat sinister smile before departing, "Of course beta, you two have fun. But not too much fun!"

I knew exactly what—or rather who—was going to be the topic of the Auntie gossip session tonight.

"Thank you for saving me."

"Anytime."

DHUM DHUM DHUM DHUM DHUMMMMM DHUM DHUM.

"Let's dance."

I lost myself in the music for a little while, getting drunk on the dhol. I couldn't feel my body, everything was sort of numb and quiet. Like all the voices had suddenly softened to a whisper. All the pressures of work had floated out of sight and out of mind. All I had to think about was moving my body to the beat. The freedom made me feel intoxicated.

I eventually pulled myself out of the dance, especially when my feet felt like they were going to spontaneously detach from my legs and I sat down with the bride to get some mehendi done myself.

"Mind if I take a seat?"

Amara smiled up at me, her porcelain skin was glowing, even more so than usual. Love always did look good on her. I'd never seen Nick so happy either, my cousin was never the romantic type. At least not until he met Amara.

"Kiara! Bless you, everyone abandoned me for the music. Turns out dhols are more interesting than the bride. I guess no-one loves me as much as they say they do,"

"Except me, of course," Nick beamed down at Amara from behind her. They locked eyes and for a moment, they looked so engrossed in each-other that I think they forgot I existed.

"Except you, *of course*," she whispered back softly.

"Time to search for my name in your mehendi, I guess," he seemed nervous.

Amara laughed, "Remember the last time I had mehendi done with your name in it? God, that feels like forever ago."

They truly had spent a lifetime together. I looked at Jai and I couldn't help the swarm of butterflies that took flight in my stomach. I wanted all that and much more for us too.

I sat patiently while mehendi was painted onto my skin, people watching.

"Would you like me to put his name in your mehendi?" The artist looked to be about my age, and she had a knowing smile on her face.

"Huh, sorry, what?" I was really out of it. I didn't even realise how many beautiful designs she'd drawn by the time I looked down at my hands. There were flowers and peacocks and swirls and dots.

She laughed softly to herself, "The one you keep staring at. I mean he keeps looking over here too, checking on you every couple minutes."

I tried not to turn an unflattering shade of cherry tomato, "His name is Jai. He's my fiancé," I said, waggling around my left hand. She grinned at me and I couldn't help but grin back.

I cleared my throat quickly and added, "Yeah, it would be nice if you could put his name somewhere in there."

.   .   .

Knock. Knock. Knock. I got up to open my door and found Jai on the other side. He shot me a grin. Something about him seemed off though. His face looked flushed and pale.

Don't overthink it. Maybe he's stressed.

"Hi,"

"Hey, you up for taking a little midnight stroll?" His voice was calm and clear but something about his eyes told me that something was wrong. The usual twinkle had dimmed, replaced by a thick cloud of stormy emotions. I felt my gut sink a little but I tried not to show it,

"Always."

We walked toward the still flower-decked beach, neither of us saying a word—the sound of our footsteps and the shifting sand filled the restless silence. He slowed to a stop and began to almost prepare himself to say something. I could feel that same sinking feeling again. Like something was gnawing at my gut, telling me this was wrong.

He took my hand in his, "Kiara, God I don't even know how to say this." His breath hitched. I wasn't sure I was breathing at all.

"Full sentences might be a good way to go about it," I whispered into the wind. We both chuckled sadly, knowing that whatever he was about to say was going to change the trajectory of our lives.

"Kiara, I'm–I–I think we should break up."

The words hit me like a ton of bricks. I thought I'd crumble, fall to pieces on the floor. I *wanted to* shatter at that moment. To escape the cruel realisation and the even more sickening discovery that after four years and an engagement, he wanted to break up with me. I pulled my hand from his, keeping my face stone-like. My eyes stung with tears, fighting to escape down my cheeks. My throat burned with bile, threatening to close up just so I wouldn't have to say anything to him. So I could just walk away.

He tried to take my hand again, "Kiara, don't be like that."

"Don't touch me."

"What was I supposed to do? Do you think my parents are happy with me marrying a girl who gets paid more than me? Who would be the main provider for our family? Who would–who would stop me from fulfilling my duties as a husband? As a father? As a man? I worked at your Father's company for years. Practically helped Dhruv build the London office from the ground up, and I still didn't get promoted to CFO. You did." His voice burned with hatred.

"I think you forget that I was right there beside all of you. That I stayed up countless nights with my Father in the office. That I never missed a single meeting, never sacrificed my job for anything else. I worked harder than all of you because I knew that I would never get the same opportunities. My Father made me CFO because he knew I could do it. Because I deserved it."

I slipped the ring off my finger and slapped it into the palm of his hand. "Have a nice life, Jai."

I pushed back the tears as I ran off the beach, keeping myself composed before I could let them fall freely. I cried alone in the dark for hours. It felt like forever before I made it to some random dock and sat down. I cried some more after that.

God I couldn't believe him. The audacity. He threw away four years and a chance at the rest of our lives together because I got the job promotion that he wanted. We'd worked together all our lives. It was coming at some point, whether it would've been me or him. How could he even do that? He was the one who encouraged me, who always said that we should grow *together*.

He's also the one who broke your heart.

All I wanted was to get out of there. I felt suffocated. Like I was stuck around people who were going to continue to pity me and gossip about me and God only knows what else. I knew I'd have to hold it together though. At least until the end of the wedding. The second Amara and Nick would finish taking their seven pheras around the mandap, I'd be in a private jet on my way back to London. Doing what I do best: disappearing. I don't think I'm going to recover from this. At least not for a while. Not for a very, very long while.

.　　.　　.

I don't know what time it was when I went back to my room. I walked around aimlessly for hours and the sun was starting to rise by the time I got back. I was a broken mess. My eyes were red and puffy, my clothes soaked through with tears and I could feel the hole gaping open in my chest. I didn't want to be the girl that turns into a shattered mess when her boyfriend breaks up with her, but he let me live under false pretences for four months. Four whole months of being CFO. Four months that I'll never be able to get back. Four years. I gave him four years of my life.

Love sucks.

I trudged back to my room and collapsed on the bed before catching a ride to Amara's house with Nick.

"Hi, thanks for picking me up."

"Hey, yeah sure no problem. You okay?"

I smiled a fake smile that wilted quickly and nodded. Words were going to be my worst enemy. I was always a sentence or two away from total collapse again. I could tell Nick understood. He stopped at an ice-cream place.

"Nick, it's nine in the morning. Ice-cream, really?"

"Duh, ice-cream for breakfast is a thing you know? Plus it *is* my wedding, so you kinda have to play by my rules."

I tried not to cringe as I walked into the ice-creamery in my t-shirt and sweats looking very battered and beat. I got a scoop of cookie dough and sat down in a booth opposite Nick.

"Kiara, what's wrong?"

I shook my head and tried to muster a small smile, "Nothing."

"Kiara, don't give me that crap. We grew up together. I'm only two years older than you, I know when something's wrong. Spill."

I sighed. People were going to find out eventually and Nick was one of the few people I didn't actually mind telling. There was always an understanding between us. He kept my secrets. And I kept his.

"Jai called off the engagement."

Shock flashed across his features for a second before he returned to neutrality again. "I am going to kill that kid." He was turning a scarlet colour.

I tried to calm him down by playing down my own emotions. I'd say I did it for myself as much as I did it for him. "It's fine, honestly. I'm fine." I tried to make my most earnest face but I'd cried to the point where my entire face felt numb and sore and puffy.

I could tell he didn't believe me but gave me my space anyway.

The rest of the day leading up to the sangeet was a blur of powders and screaming and stories and curling irons. I wanted to disappear. Just take a breather from everything. It would all be over soon and if I left early, I would regret missing Nick's wedding. I wiped away my tears and practised fake smiles in the bathroom.

Two more days. That's all. Then you can disappear.

Who knows what'll happen after those two days are over though. I have no fiancé to go back to. No wedding plans to make. Everything feels like it's changing a mile a minute and I'm struggling to keep up.

Knock. Knock. Knock. I hate that sound.

"Kiara? Are you in there?"

I checked my reflection one last time and took a deep breath in. *Smile. It's showtime.* I opened the door to find Dhruv. He looked terrible. His kurta was ruffled and his hair was a mess. His knuckles were red and there was a ripe bruise across the front of his lips where a small slit bled viciously.

"Dhruv? What the hell happened?" I whispered angrily at him. There were children around so we had to be as quiet as possible. They ran after each other under us and I smiled at them before sending them on their way. I shoved him toward an empty hallway and out towards the terrace, away from everyone else.

"I know."

"What do you mean you *know*?"

"Shut up Kiara, stop playing dumb. I know what Jai did."

I leaned against the balcony, saying nothing. There was nothing left to say. Jai made his choice, even if it hurt the both of us.

"I'm sorry," My older brother always felt things more deeply than anyone else. "If it makes you feel any better, I beat him up pretty good."

I glared in his direction and he grinned back at me, cut lip still pouring liquid red. "I sometimes wonder how you're older. You have the most stupid ideas sometimes." I cleaned up his cuts carefully and covered the bruise with concealer. "Good as new."

"Thanks."

We both sat there quietly for what felt like an eternity, allowing the whooshing wind to fill the void.

"I really am sorry, you know?" He pulled me into his arms, "You can cry if you want to. I'm not saying anything to anyone."

I couldn't help it. I broke down in his arms once more. I thought that by then my tear ducts would be run dry but I was mistaken. After a little while, I mopped up my teardrops and went back inside to fix up my makeup for the sangeet. I felt like a tangle of a human but it didn't mean I had to look like one. I put on another fake smile and went to the sangeet venue.

My favourite songs were playing at extreme volumes and everyone was dancing.

This is exactly what you need right now. Get lost in the music.

I danced until there was no-one left on the floor. I put my all into the steps we'd choreographed for Nick and Amara. There was nothing to focus on besides the music. I felt numb again. Like a soul detached from mind and body. Like a shell of a human. But it was nice. It felt freeing. Like I could finally breathe again.

My feet were numb and my head was spinning but I didn't care. I'd forgotten that everything, everyone in the world existed. It was just me, alone. Jai didn't exist. My broken heart wasn't broken. The gaping hole in my chest wasn't empty.

After that all I remember is blackness.

.   .   .

As it turns out, falling flat on a hard dancefloor hurts. I was covered in bruises when I woke up. They'd laid me flat on a sofa and Dhruv and Aria were sitting next to me.

"Hi guys."

"I guess sleeping beauty's awake." He tried to smile but the concern on his face masked everything.

"You had quite a fall there. Gave us a bit of a scare." Aria's face looked pale and white-ish, making me a little more nervous than I was to begin with.

"I did? The last thing I remember is dancing," I touched a sore spot on my head where no doubt there was a purplish bruise developing.

"Kiara, are you okay? Like really okay? You don't have to pretend. It's us."

"I'm fine, really." I got up from where I was lying down to rejoin the party. I could tell that I hadn't been out for long because everyone was still dancing through the night. I was aching to rejoin the wedding party, if only to get away from Dhruv and Aria's incessant questioning. They might be my brother and his wife but they'll never understand.

I knew I'd have to tell my parents at some point though. It had to be that night. I'd wait for everything to quiet down and then I'd drop the news. Like ripping off a band-aid. Easy. Right?

•   •   •

I think band-aids were a bad example. A terrible example. Breaking the news of your engagement being called off to your parents is nothing like a band-aid. In fact, it's the opposite of a band-aid. It's like trying to rip a brick away from drying cement.

"Hi guys," I walked into their room. They were both sitting on the bed on their respective phones, tapping away aggressively.

"Hi beta, what's up?"

I felt nauseous. Like everything was coming up. Except, I had nothing left in my body to throw up. I hadn't eaten anything besides ice-cream in thirty-six hours.

"I'm just going to say this quickly. Jai broke up with me last night."

My parents dropped their phones beside them and stared at me with the most shock I'd ever seen them display, "What?"

"Jai-broke-up-with-me.He-called-off-the-engagement. Don't-be-angry-that-I-waited-to-tell-you, I-was-just-looking-for-the-right-time." Everything was coming out of my mouth at a million miles per minute and in strings of sentence-long words. Ripping off a band-aid. Not quick. And definitely not painless.

My Mum took a deep breath in, "It's fine. It'll be fine."

.   .   .

Chapter 2

Kiara

Desiderium

noun

1. an ardent desire or longing; especially: a feeling of loss or grief for something lost

.   .   .

I stayed true to my word. Only God and I know how I survived the last three days, but at least I'm in the air and that much closer to London now. Just a few more hours of flying and I'll be back to the confines of my house. My sanctuary. The news has probably already made its rounds around London though. I can already see the headlines, 'Kiara Shah and Jai Gupta call off engagement; what does this mean for the future of Shah Enterprises?'

Buzz buzz. Buzz buzz. Buzz buzz.

"Hello?"

"Hi beta," my Dad's voice rumbled through the speakerphone.

"Hi Dad," I tried to sound chipper for my Dad but I could tell I was failing miserably. It'd only been about three days since the break-up but I think my parents were somewhat expecting me to bounce back already. Sponges. Miserable, miserable sponges.

"How're you holding up?"

"I'm okay. Heading back to London right now. Tell Dhruv to check his emails, I'll probably be anger-bombing him for the next couple days."

My Dad stifled a sigh but I could tell that seeing me like this was hurting him, "Why don't you take a few days off? I'm sure Dhruv and I can hold down the fort for a couple of days."

"No, I think the best thing right now is for me to go back to work and just act like nothing happened."

"The audacity of that boy. Especially after everything we did for him. I have half a mind to fire him. I'm holding off for now because no good decisions come from places of anger."

"It's okay Dad. I need a couple of days though. I just need to stay out of sight and out of mind."

Dad remained awfully quiet for a minute before saying, "I'll talk to you soon. Message us on the group chat when you land."

"I will. Love you, bye."

Jeeves, my Driver/Butler was waiting for me at the airport when I landed. Besides my Brother and Dad, Jeeves has been the most consistent man in my life. His real name is James Hunter but we call him Jeeves. I don't know why we call him Jeeves, all I know is that I've been calling him Jeeves for as long as I can remember.

"Hi Jeeves, how we doing my man?" I like breaking out my least formal English with Jeeves—I'm talking about the stuff that my New York friends teach me—just to see how he'll react. He's always a perfect gentleman though, so I'm not sure why I torture him. I guess it's just our thing.

"Good evening Ms. Shah, I am very well thank you. May I take your bags?" Jeeves is an absolute sweetheart. He drove me home.

I couldn't stop myself from thinking during the car ride though. The 'what-ifs' were taking up too much brain space. Imagine what my life would've been like if Jai and I did get married, would he have spent our entire marriage resenting me? Would we have eventually split? What if I hadn't got the promotion, then what? Would we have been happy? I can't help but think that maybe this split was for the best. If he didn't want to grow with me, then our relationship would have suffered. *I* would've suffered.

You'll be okay. Eventually. Maybe.

I showered, changed out of my airport clothes and got into bed. I couldn't sleep the entire night. I'd done the whole emotions thing. I'd gone through all the stages of being sad, angry, numb, sad again and I was beginning to feel numb again. Maybe being numb is better. At least that way I wouldn't feel the gaping hole where my heart used to be.

·   ·   ·

I didn't sleep a wink the whole night which means only one thing. Coffee. Lots and lots and lots of coffee.

No more wallowing. You have to get over it at some point.

I got out of bed and made my way to my favourite coffee shop. If anything, it would at least serve as a little pick-me-up and get me through the work day. London's weather was finally thawing out a little for summer, with the sun peeking out behind two slightly angry clouds. The weather seemed to be mimicking my mood quite well. I could feel my heart slowly beginning to repair itself but the clouds got just a little heavier and stormier as I took in the break-up piece by piece. I ordered my usual Hazelnut Cappuccino before retreating to a corner of the shop where I hoped no-one would notice me. Turns out my efforts were worthless.

"Kiara? Is that you?" Of course, on my first day back in the city I'd have to run into my least favourite person on the planet. Sanya and I went to school together and we always hated each-other's guts. Just one of those people you don't get along with.

The people that you do get along with aren't exactly proving to be much better.

"Hi Sanya, you look well."

"Well of course I do, it's me!" She said that in a manner that insinuated that I was supposed to know exactly what was going on in her life. Or care enough to ask.

I just laughed awkwardly.

"So, darling, are you okay?" She lowered her voice to a whisper, like we were sharing some sort of super-secret. She was practically bubbling with excitement.

"I'm doing great, thanks for asking." A complete and total lie, but she didn't need to know that,

She almost laughed as she erupted, "Are you sure? I heard you and Jai broke up. He called off your engagement, right?"

She tried to keep her face straight but I could see the sheer joy flashing across her features. I let some amount of panic burn across my face before I returned a cold smile. I had no clue what I was going to say next.

"We need some time to explore our careers right now." What? It's not like I was lying. We were spending time exploring our careers, I just left out the part where I gave him the ring back and cried for three days straight.

She smiled a sinister smile and opened her mouth to say something before she was interrupted, "Hazelnut Cappuccino for Kiara, I have a hazelnut cappuccino for Kiara." Saved by the bell.

"I guess the coffee calls. I'll see you around Sanya." With that, I grabbed my coffee and got out of the coffee shop as quickly as humanly possible.

I thought I'd be safe. It's only been about seventy-six hours since we broke up but I guess news travels fast in our circles.

Ding. Ding. Ding.

2 new messages from Mama.

I opened my phone.

12:28
Hi meri jaan
How are you holding up?
Hi Mama
I'm okay
Guess who I just bumped into
Well less bumped and more crashed
Who?
Sanya
Oh gosh
What happened? What did she say this time?
She knows about the break-up
Which means that everyone knows

Buzz buzz buzz.

"Hi Mama."

My Mum took a deep breath, as if preparing to send me off to war. She isn't exactly overreacting. When things like this arise in our social circles, it's like going to war. There's a very small circle of people like us in London which means that everyone is constantly watching everyone, hunting for weaknesses. It only takes one brick for the entire wall to come tumbling down. Everything felt like a pile of rubble anyway, what was left to save?

"Hi Kiara. So you saw Sanya, what exactly did she say to you?"

"She was asking about the break-up, she knew exactly what went down. It was as if she was at the break-up. Like someone gave her a simultaneous play-by-play of our entire night. She knew that I'd given the ring back and that *he* broke up with *me*."

My Mum sighed softly, trying to hide her frustration from me. "What's done is done now. The best part is that you sound okay, *are you okay my darling*?" She lowered her voice to a whisper. Her usual Mum way of checking on me. Like even if I wasn't okay, it was a secret just between the two of us. No-one else had to know.

"I'm…I don't know what I am. But I do know that I will eventually be okay. Or at least okay-adjacent."

"Of course you will be, you're my sher bachha. The first female CFO of Shah Enterprises and the youngest person to be made CFO. If anyone is going to get over this quickly, it's you."

I laughed softly. "Dad and Dhruv are suggesting that I take some time off. Maybe it's not a bad idea. Everyone here practically knows anyway and I'd rather not be here so they can freely bombard me with questions and care baskets and fake pity. Should I take a quick trip and come back?"

I could hear the smile in her voice as she replied, "If it feels like something you want to do, then go for it." The smile disappeared, "But if you're only going to try to run away from your problems, then don't."

"I'll think about it for a little longer. I'll talk to you later. Love you Mama, bye."

"Bye baby. Love you."

.   .   .

Buzz. Buzz. Buzz.

Ding. Ding. Ding.

Whoosh. Whoosh. Whoosh.

Ring. Ring. Ring.

That's what my phone sounded like for the entire next two days. I was tempted to just smash it to pieces so that no-one could contact me. Or just turn it off permanently and get a new phone with a new number. People were bombarding me with phone calls to 'check-in' on me—I learnt quickly that the majority of those phone calls were nosy family members that wanted the inside scoop on what was apparently the break-up of the century—hundreds of text messages, emails, DM's, Snaps. You name it and people tried it. My kitchen looked like a florist had just dumped an entire flower field and left. My entire second fridge was stocked with boxes of chocolates. The same Patchi and Godiva boxes that everyone deemed appropriate for major heartbreak. While I appreciated the sentiment, I just wanted to deal with things on my own. Privately.

I don't think the media is aware of the meaning of the term private. There were articles everyday, the headlines exactly as I predicted.

I spent the rest of the day thinking about vacation destinations. Yes, I'm avoiding my problems a little bit but I also deserve a vacation. I think it's clear that the phone, flower and chocolate parade isn't ending anytime soon. Besides, I haven't taken a holiday in three years because I've been working my arse off to make CFO. My Dad did say that he needed someone to go and get the Dubai office set up for a few months. That job would be perfect for me. I wouldn't have work withdrawal symptoms because I'd still be working the entire time and I'd be able to get out of London until everything blows over. Win-win-win.

I shot my Dad and Dhruv an email to explain everything and I started packing my bags. I'd been to Dubai a couple times when I was younger but the city had progressed so much since I'd last been there. If I wanted to get out of London, what better place than Dubai, right? By the time I reached the airport, I'd read everything there was to read about it. Practically fallen in love with the city through the magazine pages. Things were starting to look up, at least a little bit.

Chapter 3

Kiara

Ambedo

noun

1. a kind of melancholic trance in which you become completely absorbed in vivid sensory details

.   .   .

After two days of packing, contemplating, unpacking and repacking, I made my way to the airport. I'm not exactly the most decisive person, so I went back on my decision four different times before I got to the airport. Even then, I was tempted to miss my flight and just stay home. As much as it sounded like a good idea two days ago when all the Indians in London were bombarding me with calls and presents and messages, did I really want to go? I'm comfortable in London. It's where I've grown up. All my family is here, my friends, my house, Jeeves; I didn't know if I was really prepared to give all that up for a few months. It's not like a holiday where I go for a couple of days and come back. I have to stay there until the office is up and running, which could take weeks, months even.

What's the worst that could happen though?

Something was telling me to go for it though. Like some part of me knew exactly how the story would unravel, even if I didn't. It didn't sound rational to suddenly pack up my entire life because of one stupid break-up but no-one said that heartbroken people are rational people. That hole in my chest felt like it was healing with each minute on the drive towards the airport. I said my goodbyes to Jeeves and boarded the jet.

I spent seven hours scrutinising the last four years of my life. Every decision I'd made. I needed to slowly phase Jai out from the corners of my world and that would start with social media. I opened my phone and started looking through my Instagram. I didn't post very often, but when I did, it was almost always with Jai. I don't believe in deleting anything. I think once a person is part of your life, it should stay that way. He was a big part of my life for four years and that can't just suddenly be erased. I decided not to do anything to the pictures of us in the snow, or at dinner, or riding jet skis during the summer. They all served as memories of who I used to be, but they don't dictate who I will become without him. Instead of removing them, I decided to add something new. I took a picture of my window—the rosy sunset blending into a star stricken midnight blue thousands of feet above the earth—and posted it. The caption: new beginnings.

Buzz buzz. Buzz buzz. Buzz buzz.

Amara wants to Facetime you.

I answered to find a swimsuit-clad Amara, sipping coconut water on a sandy beach in some corner of the Maldives.

"You look awfully comfy there don't you cuz." I couldn't help but smile at the sight of her. She looked happier than ever.

"Hi! Yeah it's great. No work emails. No phone calls. No messages. I am a *free bird*. What's up with you? Are you—are you in a *plane*?!" She squinted her eyes at the screen as if it would help her make out my location.

I laughed, I guess I have been awfully detached from everyone lately. "Yeah, I'm on a plane. On my way to Dubai. Just needed to get out of London for a bit. Things were getting…a bit much."

She smiled consolingly, "I heard. He's a jerk."

There was a near awkward pause where she and I were trying to figure out whether or not to actually acknowledge the break-up. It felt like the length of a microwave minute but I'm convinced it was only about thirty seconds.

"Wait, I have a great idea. Why don't Nick and I come visit you on our way home? We'll make a pit stop in Dubai for a couple days. It's a win-win. We can help you get settled and we get a little extra vacation." She looked over at her husband and chuckled. "He's fast asleep right now," she turned the camera toward him to show me, "But I'm sure he'll be really excited once I can get him to wake up. He's spent the last three days in the exact same position, you know." His face was covered with a giant sun hat and his gangly limbs were tangled awkwardly on the pool lounger.

"Sounds good. I'll see you guys in a couple days then?"

"Definitely. Fly safe. We miss you."

.   .   .

The first thing I noticed when I touched down was the heat. What was I expecting, the middle of the dessert to be frozen like the tundra? Mistake number 1—and counting—was bringing my London-weather appropriate clothing.

Guess I'll have to go shopping. Not a bad mistake actually.

It was boiling outside. I could feel my frozen body thawing out in the Dubai warmth. Exactly what I needed. The drive on the way to the house was invigorating. I didn't realise how hungry I was to see the city. It was miles of skyscrapers and lights and extravagant cars, quiet deserts and buzzing streets. All I had to do was get through one more night. Then I could explore everything.

.   .   .

Ring. Ring. Ring.

"Hi Kiara, good morning my cutie pie!" My Mum always chooses to wake me up in the most sugar coated ways. I guess it makes early mornings just that much easier.

I answered Facetime but continued sleeping.

"Mmmmm,"

She laughed, "Rise or shine, you'll miss the entire day."

"Mhmmm, just five more minutes."

"I know you're tired but if you don't want to miss the entire day, now is probably a good time to wake up sweetheart."

I grunted loudly, "Fine. I'm up." I stared into my reflection on the phone screen. I looked like an absolute mess. My hair was tangled and dishevelled and my clothes were definitely nowhere near presentable. I got up, placed the phone on the counter near the sink and started brushing my teeth. My Mum caught me up on all the drama after the wedding. Apparently the Aunties had a field day when they heard we'd broken up. They were battering my parents with questions and 'concerned' suggestions. All the Aunties with unmarried daughters were using my break-up as an opportunity to find their daughters a husband.

Pink Auntie had all sorts of questions for my Mum, "So, what kind of food does he like? How much does he get paid? Is his position at the company secure? Does he want a girl who's good at cooking and cleaning?" Turns out she's looking for a husband for her daughter Tara. I couldn't help but laugh a little when my Mum told me all this. Pinky Auntie really is one of a kind. According to my Mother, I'm quite high in demand as well. The news of me being off the market struck up a plethora of interest from all the single Desi men and their parents in our circle. Though I'm willing to bet that the parents are far more interested in me than their sons are. My parents had already had close to a hundred marriage proposals come in. She read through a couple of them,

"Bunty Singh, aged 24, works at Google, is a feminist."

"Dev Anand, aged 23, works at DIFC, a big supporter of the feminist movement."

Now duplicate that application but change the names, ages and jobs. What's the common factor? Feminism. Pretty much every single application mentioned that the candidate was a feminist. I guess Desi's do really love to learn from other people's mistakes.

After about half an hour of primping and prodding at my face, I looked just about decent enough to leave my room.

"Bye Mama. Talk soon."

With that, I was off. I took my rental Tesla down to the new office building. I'd been to Dubai a few times before but not since I was a teenager. Thankfully, Mum and Dad decided to keep their holiday home here for a little bit longer. They were considering selling it last year because no-one had come up in a while but I convinced them not to. It seemed like an investment worth keeping. Technically I wasn't supposed to go up to the office on the first day in the city, but I'm too much of a workaholic. It would continue to bother me until I at least figured out where it was and got my bearings with the surrounding area. I always need to find a good coffee shop nearby, otherwise surviving the working day becomes almost unbearable. I drove around the city for a little while, getting lost and found every few minutes. The office building was beautiful. The entire place was covered in floor to ceiling windows and homed a coffee shop, juice bar and mini supermarket. There were also a ton of vending machines stocked with the best snacks and drinks. The building was empty. It wouldn't be fair of me to expect there to be anyone working on a Saturday but then again not everyone is me. I scoured around the office, taking in the cubicles—decorated with family photos, sticky notes and overflowing with papers—and closed offices. The space was airy and full of light: exactly the way I like it.

I've seen it. I guess I should go now. Go and actually explore the city. Alone.

I was feeling a little bit lonelier than usual. I usually spend Saturday's with Jai. We would order in breakfast sandwiches, walk down to our favorite coffee shop to grab cappuccinos and spend the rest of the day roaming around London. My parents always had family dinners and game nights on Saturday's so we'd spend our nights there, arguing with Dhruv and Aria about who actually won Monopoly or forcing my Mum to let us help her in the kitchen. I hadn't spent a Saturday alone in a while.

A very, very, very long while.

I got back into the Tesla and opened my Notes app to look at the list of spots I'd made for myself:

Dubai Mall. I wouldn't mind a shopping trip right about now. I've heard that retail therapy is great for break-ups. Plus, I desperately needed some summer wear. My London-wear was not going to cut it any longer.

I typed Dubai Mall into Waze and set off. Twenty minutes later, I was in shopping heaven. I spent hours and hours and hours shopping. By the end of it, I'd made three trips to the car and had consumed two coffees and multiple different snacks and desserts. I came home with an entire wardrobe and was so well distracted I forgot about the entire break-up thing until I got a message later on in the evening. It was from Jai.

God this man doesn't want me to live in peace. Don't answer. But what if it's something important?

I spent the entire car ride home debating whether or not to respond.

Delivered. That's definitely the easiest way.

I unpacked my new wardrobe when I got back to the house and started to put together my outfit for dinner. This is one of the few work type things that I have to do before work in the office actually starts on Monday. I'm meeting the guy who's supposedly running the Dubai office, that is once I help him get it set up. I'm not even sure what his name is actually. Maybe I should've checked on that before agreeing to dinner with him.

Nice going Kiara. He could be some random serial killer.

Serial killer or not, I was going to this dinner. He'd booked us a table at Zuma and I couldn't be any happier. I'd had a ton of snacks throughout the day but my body was practically begging for a proper meal after all that shopping.

Hmmm. Do I go with the black dress or the red? Black or red? I can't decide. Maybe I shouldn't.

I Facetimed the one person who I knew would be perfect at helping me decide.

"Aria!"

She smiled at me through the phone, "Kiara! What's up crazy lady?"

I mock scowled, "I can't decide on a dress and I need help. Desperately." I turned my phone around to show her the long black dress and the strapless red mini dress I'd bought earlier in the day.

"Hmmm…I do love them both, but I'm thinking black. The red is incredible but maybe a little too bold for a business dinner. Plus, you can never go wrong with an LBD."

Perfect. Black it is.

"See, I knew I could trust you to help me decide." I set my phone down on the vanity in my bedroom.

She laughed, "So, I haven't heard from you in a couple days. We missed you at game night." Her smile dimmed a little and I could feel my facial features go limp.

"Anyway, what're we thinking for hair and makeup?" She tried to brighten the mood a little again.

I spoke to Aria all whilst getting ready and then I was out the door for dinner. I settled on the long black dress, blown out hair and subtle makeup. Demure but authoritative. Or at least that's what Aria said.

.   .   .

Kabir

This is going to be an easy night. Just a quick dinner and you're done.

I'd been convincing myself to feel some level of excitement to go to dinner that night with Key-ra, Ki-ra, Kee-ya-ra, however it is you say her name. I didn't need anyone to come in and help me set up my office. I'm perfectly capable of doing it on my own. Those were the exact words I'd used when Dhruv called me a couple days ago announcing her trip. I didn't prod any further because he's her brother. And also my boss. It's a big 'also'. I know.

Last I'd seen her she was an experience-hungry teenager. I couldn't stand to be around her.

Don't be an arse. She was never that bad.

Allow me to rephrase myself. I can't stand to be around anyone. I don't like people. I'm not a people person. It's just one dinner. Maybe it won't be quite as bad.

I buttoned up my suit, gave my hair one last look in the mirror and locked my front door. The drive to Zuma was quick and painless.

At least part of my night will be quick and painless.

That's part of what I love about living downtown; everything is so unbelievably accessible. Work is just a few minutes from my apartment, so are my favorite restaurants, the Dubai Mall and the best bars. Quick and Painless. Exactly the way I like it.

I got to the restaurant a couple minutes early so I could make the rounds. Beside my apartment, the gym and work, I spent the most amount of time at Zuma. Business dinners were practically my entire life. I said a quick hello to the managers and chefs, all of whom I'd developed a sort of kinship with over the years. Like I said, I come here a lot.

I sat down at my usual table and waited. Dinner was supposed to start at nine PM but I had a feeling we wouldn't be starting till about nine thirty. Women are almost always late. Typical.

I was just getting comfortable when a woman, about 5'2, approached the table.

"Yes?"

"Hi, I'm Kiara."

Eye-ra, so that's how you say it. *I wasn't far off.*

I got up, "Hi, I'm Kabir. Please, take a seat." I gestured to the empty seat across from me. I tried to hide the slight shock flashing over my features as I got a decent look at her.

She's gorgeous.

I cleared my throat, "So Kiara, how're you enjoying Dubai so far?"

She smiled, "It's only my first day here but it's been amazing so far."

This is going to be a very boring night.

.   .   .

Kiara

This is going to be a very long night.

I entered the restaurant to find a presumably Indian man sitting at a lone table overlooking downtown Dubai. I walked up to the table and the first words to come out of his mouth were, "Yes?"

Can you believe it? "Yes?" And not even the polite kind of "Yes?", it was very much a 'what are *you* doing here?' type of "Yes?"

I tried my best not to look horrified, "Hi, I'm Kiara."

He stood up quickly but kept a cool and calculated mask on his face. So he's one of *those* guys, interesting. Very interesting. "Hi, I'm Kabir."

So he is Indian.

He then proceeded to ask me about my stay in Dubai. Typical. He doesn't even know how to make interesting conversation.

"So, Kabir, tell me about yourself." If I'm going to be spending the next couple weeks here, I need to know exactly who I'm up against.

The corners of his lips lifted ever so slightly, as if he knew exactly what I was thinking. I'd known him only ten minutes but he was already making the blood heat under the surface of my skin.

Maybe it's because he's astonishingly handsome.

"I grew up here. Went to LSE and now I work for your company."

"The details are riveting."

He scoffed softly, "You'll find soon that I'm not all that interesting." He kept up that cool mask, his features staying taut and precise.

I guess I know what I'm up against now, and I'm not sure I like it.

I needed to get the conversation back on more civil terms. And quickly.

"So tell me, what are the spots I definitely need to visit while I'm here?"

Something in his eyes changed from cold and detached to warm and connected. "You might want to get your Notes app out for this,"

I opened my phone and noted down all the places as he called them out. "Thanks."

"No problem. Let me know if you need any more suggestions.

.   .   .

Kabir

I couldn't help but be slightly ecstatic when she called it an early night. I desperately wanted to escape. She spent forty minutes sizing me up as if I were some mountain she was figuring out how to climb. Dinner was relatively civil. Just about as civil as it can be between two people who hardly know each other and are essentially at war. Or at least I was going to war. Whether she knew about it or not.

Ring. Ring. Ring.

"Hello?"

"Hi hon," My Mum sounded like she was practically going to fly off her seat before exploding with questions about dinner. "How was dinner?"

There it is. I laughed softly, "It was good."

"What's she like? Come on, give me some details."

I tried to come up with a clear image of her in my head but I couldn't seem to find a single one where I hadn't mentally drawn on devil horns and a tail with red marker. "She's—she's nice."

"She's nice," what a lie.

"Good, good. Have you offered to take her around yet?" My parents were desperate for me to find a girlfriend. Who better in their eyes than my extremely powerful (*and beautiful*) boss, Kiara Shah. My Mum was probably the only person on the planet excited to find out that she and her fiancé called it quits. Ever since then it's been 'Operation Get Kabir Married' on full speed. In simple terms, the past few days have been hell.

"No, I haven't. She's a grown woman. I'm sure she can get around by herself."

"Stop being stupid Kabir. This is your chance, don't waste it."

"I'll think about it Mum. Talk to you tomorrow."

"Okay hon. Good night. Love you."

"Love you."

Should I be offering to take her around? It might earn me some brownie points with the rest of the Chief Executive team. Then again, I don't know how long I'll be able to stand her.

You have to do this.

I opened up my phone to message her.

12:37
Hey
If you want, I wouldn't mind showing you around the city.
We could meet tomorrow morning for breakfast, say 10?
Hi
Yeah sure, that would be cool
I'll see you tomorrow at 10

Kiara

Agreeing to that was such a terrible idea. Why in the world would I agree to letting him show me around the city?

Because he's very attractive.

I opened up Instagram to find out exactly what this guy was all about. Social media is always the best way to figure out exactly who someone is. I started scrolling through. *Gym picture. Gym picture. Wedding picture. Beach picture. Gym picture.*

Wait, a wedding picture. Interesting. I opened up the post to find a carousel of pictures from a wedding. He was standing with a girl in the first picture. They look awfully close to be just friends. Maybe he's taken. My cheeks heated at the thought.

Why do you care anyway? You can't stand him.

It doesn't matter. All I know is that I'm meeting him for breakfast tomorrow. It's just breakfast. Maybe it won't be that bad.

·   ·   ·

Chapter 4

Kiara

Early mornings are not my thing. Especially when I don't have someone to wake me up gently four different times. I hit the snooze button on my alarm seven different times before I finally managed to make it out of my bed. Alarms are so condescending.

I got ready and clambered into my Tesla, ready to face the city once more. We were meeting at Yamanote Atelier, one of the spots I'd made note of in my list. I couldn't wait to explore the bakery. The custard pie was practically calling my name. I made it to DIFC and strolled through for a little while before arriving at my destination. It was packed. I'm talking sardines in a tin can packed.

I sat down at a little table outside and ordered myself a matcha latte while I waited. At around ten thirty, I got a message from Kabir saying that he'd be a little late. Typical. Men think they can just waltz in at any time and we'll remain begging at their feet. I was tempted to get up and leave but that wouldn't look good.

You know what would look good? His head on a platter.

It's not exactly a positive sign if we start bickering almost immediately. I have to figure out how to be cordial with him sooner rather than later. Especially before either of us does something foolish. Otherwise, the next couple weeks are going to be unbearable.

Quick and painless. Let's just make this quick and painless.

I expected him to walk in with at least a mild level of urgency considering that he was an entire forty-seven minutes late, but this man sashayed in as if he had all the time in the world. I could feel my blood beginning to heat again.

"You're late."

"Good morning to you too," he tried to keep his features in that usual icy mask of his but I could see him wince slightly as he walked up to me.

I took a deep breath. *There's no point in being mad. If you show him you're angry, he wins. Forget him, enjoy the city.*

"You wanna order something?" I smiled, forcefully stretching my lips into a thin grin.

"You haven't lived until you've had their custard pie."

I walked into the restaurant and I couldn't help but practically sigh at the smell of sugar and caffeine and tea leaves. The bakery was stocked with pastries and sandwiches and cakes and cookies. "Can I have a minion bun, two custard pies, and a mini French toast boat please?"

I practically ordered the entire menu, but I couldn't help myself. It all looked too good. Between the peaceful outdoor seating at DIFC and the smell of sugar, spice and everything nice inside the bakery, I felt myself falling deeper in love with the city. More so than I already had.

Imagine living here.

We sat down at our table once more. "So what's the plan for today?"

He smiled, "Today is going to be one of the best days of your life."

I rolled my eyes at his comment.

Best day of my life. Puh-lease.

"We'll start our morning off at La Mer. Please tell me you brought a swimsuit." He winced a little as if worried by whatever response I was about to dish out.

He's so unbelievably unprepared. He didn't even tell me what to wear or what to bring with me. Thankfully, I kept a swimsuit, towel, change of clothes and snacks in the car at all times.

"What kind of activity requires a swimsuit?"

"The best kind, obviously."

The gleam in his eyes made me a little bit worried.

By that time the custard pies, minion bun and french toast had all arrived. I tried to stifle another sigh at the smell of powdered sugar and vanilla but failed miserably.

"The way you're looking at the custard pie right now would make any sane man think you haven't had a meal in days."

I scoffed, "What does that make you then?"

"I'm…half-sane," the ghost of a smile wafted around his lips for a moment before disappearing into that same frost tipped mask.

I took a bite of the custard pie, and for a moment I felt almost lost in the world of sugar, vanilla and flaky pastry. I love food a little too much for my own good. It's one of the best desserts I've had in my entire life.

I could feel his eyes burning into my skull as I devoured the rest of the custard pie. I tried not to wither under his stare but the pressure felt like a ten kilo weight. I got the rest of my bakery items as a takeaway and we set off.

"So are we taking my car or yours?"

"Let's take mine. You can drive. I'm used to being passenger princess anyway."

.   .   .

Kabir

Passenger princess?

What the hell is she talking about? I stifled my curiosity and decided not to ask in the case that it sparked up an endless debate between us. That's the last thing I need right now. I'm going to show her the city, stack up all the brownie points and then get her out of my hair.

I tried not to gape a little when I saw her car. As much as she frustrates every facet of my being, the girl has decent taste.

"Nice car."

"Thanks."

I barely managed to squeeze myself into the car without spraining my knees. "God, you're tiny." I mumbled under my breath.

"What was that?"

I tried not to turn red at my accidental admission, "No I was just saying that I have to adjust the seat a little."

I pushed the seat back as far as possible to make room for my legs. There's a decent amount of difference between 5'2 and 6'2, I realize that now. I could feel her staring at me as I adjusted myself.

The drive was long, awkward and somewhat quiet. I would try to make conversation every few minutes by pointing out a building or landmark, but she sat there nodding and taking pictures like a mime. I didn't blame her. It's not like I'd been the most polite up until now.

I could see her eyes light up a little as we got to La Mer.

"That's La Mer, I pointed from across the road as we walked in."

"It's beautiful," she took in everything, almost breathing in all the different senses. I would too if I got to experience Dubai for the first time all over again.

I pointed my finger upwards at the giant water park slide, "And that, right there is what we'll be tackling today."

Yes, I'm taking her to a water park. And yes, even seemingly grumpy workaholics like water parks.

"I didn't know you were capable of enjoying something as convivial as a water park."

I tried my hardest not to smirk, "I'm capable of a lot more than you'd think."

Her cheeks flushed a little and I couldn't help but feel a certain sense of triumph at the biology of winning this conversation. I nodded towards the changing rooms, "Go get changed. I'll meet you out here."

I waited a few minutes until she changed into a swimsuit and clambered back out, "So what're we tackling first?"

I smiled a little wickedly and led her straight to the biggest slide. The park was buzzing with life. The stairs up to the slide felt endless, even for someone who goes to the gym as often as I do. I could tell she was beginning to get tired as we made our way up the second flight with two more to go. Her breathing was getting increasingly ragged and she was huffing and puffing everywhere. I tried not to laugh.

·　　　·　　　·

Kiara

God these stairs are endless. `

It was getting harder and harder to breathe as we walked further and further up. *Maybe I need to start working out more.* I probably should work out a little more often. I stopped for a minute to catch my breath and looked around. I could see the entirety of La Mer from up there. The beach was teeming with life. Surfers cutting through waves, children building crumbling sandcastles and people strolling along the boardwalk. It felt like a beach straight out of a movie scene. Most cities aren't capable of having such a cosmopolitan downtown scene with a California-rivalling beach just twenty minutes away from each other. *It's incredible.*

"Come on, we have to keep going up the stairs."

I groaned and continued to climb up even with the lactic acid making my legs practically immobile. We made it to the top of the stairs and were greeted by an extremely enthusiastic ride conductor, "Hey guys, how are you?"

I tried to smile through the pain, "We're good."

He gestured to the circular pool at the top of the ride where a giant circular ring was placed, "Hop in carefully."

I gulped, *we have to do this together?*

He got into the ring first and I got in after, my legs brushed against his and I could feel him recoiling at the touch. My cheeks heated.

The conductor let the ring go into the ride. We entered a big circular tunnel, where everything went pitch black. I tried to keep my hands to myself and firmly gripped on the bands around the side of the ring. Then suddenly, we were free falling.

"AHHHHHHHHHHHH!" I couldn't help but scream.

He started laughing beside me, watching me through some sort of superiority complex drive microscope. I'd never even seen him smile before, but his laugh was practically exhilarating. It sounded rough and coarse, like it was rarely put into practice—yet somehow sweet at the same time. I tried not to grin back at him but folded anyway. We swooped from side to side in this giant bowl and I continued to switch between screaming and laughing while he watched me with wide eyes. By the end of the ride, we were both somewhat giddy.

Maybe he's not so bad after all.

We did a couple more rides and climbed countless more flights of those awful stairs before calling it quits. "Where to next?"

"You'll just have to wait and see."

That sentence makes me nervous. It sounds like something a nice random man with candy says before it turns out that he's a serial killer. It's not like I have much of a choice though, so I went along with it. We started to drive past downtown Dubai and I couldn't help but be in awe of the entire place. The streets were lined with fluttering palm trees, the buildings were shiny, restaurants dotted the entire main street and people were clearly enjoying themselves. I wanted to stay there forever. I probably would've if I had the option. Instead, I took a picture, so I could keep that moment forever.

We pulled into Souk Al Bahar for lunch. We walked to the Time Out Market, which was one of the spots I had on my list. I didn't realise how hungry I'd be until we walked in and the aroma of a million different things blasted me on the face. The place looked incredible. The lights were slightly dimmed and the market was full of restaurants. All the kitchens were open and the menus were on little signs right below the restaurant name. Small tables lined the back of every restaurant and posters were plastered across the walls.

I think I'm in heaven.

"Okay so, there's a million different things to try. I've tried all of them, but I have to say that Pitfire Pizza is the best."

I nodded, "Let's get some pizza then."

I tried not to groan as I took a bite of the garlic knots we ordered. I didn't realise how much I needed food until greasy, carb-loaded garlicky goodness dipped in even more garlic hit my lips. Kabir looked at me like I was a crazy person. The pure revulsion on his face made me want to slap him.

That does seem fun.

"What?"

"Nothing, nothing."

I tried my hardest not to ask him to elaborate, partially because I probably wasn't ready for whatever unnecessarily harsh truth he was going to give me in return, and partially because if I seem curious, he wins, and I'm always the winner.

It was only lunch-time but we were already running out of things to talk about—or at least things that wouldn't spark hours of intense debates and potentially catastrophic arguments. The conversations were getting more awkward by the minute.

"So, tell me about yourself."

"I thought we covered that last night."

I tried not to laugh as I remembered his response from the other night, "Give me the long version this time."

A phantom smile played on his lips, "I was born here. Both my parents are Indian but they moved here about twenty five years ago. Being born here was probably the best thing that could've ever happened to me. I've travelled the entire world—my parents made sure of it—but there's really no place that I'd be happier to call home." The glitter in his eyes when he talked about Dubai made me want to know more. "I went to school here and then went to LSE for uni. I loved the UK and my time there because it's when I started working for your Dad, but I missed Dubai and my parents too much. I always knew I would move back, so when your Dad decided to set up the Dubai office, I knew I was the man for the job. The timing was perfect so I decided to leave London and settle down here again. That's pretty much my life until this point."

I tried not to smile. As rude and condescending as he may seem, I think he actually has a heart.

I nodded, trying to fill the quiet in the air. He wiped his face with a tissue and looked up at me. It was only then that I noticed the chiselled nature of his jaw, his milky brown eyes and rosy cheeks.

He's handsome.

"Now that you know all about me, I think it's only fair that you tell me about yourself too."

.   .   .

Kabir

I'm so stupid. Why would I even ask that?

Admit it. You like her. You want to know more.

She hesitated for a minute, like she really had to think about what to say. The pause made me even more curious, what's with the need to be calculated?

"I was born and brought up in London but I've travelled the entire globe. My parents were always big globetrotters so they took me pretty much everywhere under the sun. I studied at Cambridge and then started working for my Dad's company. Got promoted to CFO a couple months ago. I think that pretty much sums me up."

Convenient. She left out the part about her fiancé. Ex-fiancé. I mean, I would too. I know, it's awfully human of me, but I sort of sympathise. I've never really had a serious relationship, so I wouldn't know the first thing about being heartbroken, but I understand the feeling of loneliness.

Maybe a little too well.

We finished the last of our food before moving onto our next destination. I was debating where to take her. Dubai has so much to offer that it's difficult to decide where to go. I've lived here all my life and I still haven't covered everything.

It was only about three o'clock in the afternoon but I wanted to fit in a couple more spots before we called it a night.

Why are you trying so hard? You definitely like her.

"How do you feel about fish?"

Am I stupid or something? Who asks a question like that?

"I like them?"

I brought her to the Dubai Aquarium. It's been one of my favourite places ever since I was a little kid. My parents used to bring me all the time, and we used to make a little day out of it. We'd grab ice-cream and then take a walk around the aquarium before my Mum usually dragged us around the rest of the mall.

"Two tickets please."

We walked through the underwater tunnel. Fish were flitting to and fro. I'd imagine it's how they describe the ocean in kids books, making it seem as magical as possible. I could see sharks and stingrays and schools of hundreds of fish. It made me feel like a little kid again. Nostalgia.

Kiara had her eyes glued to the walls, she was checking out every feature on every fish that she saw. Her lips would curve into a smile or curl up into an 'o' every time she saw something even remotely captivating. Seeing things through her eyes somehow made me appreciate them even more. Sometimes a fresh perspective can do wonders.

Maybe it's just her *perspective.*

I laughed silently as we walked through the aquarium. She'd stop every few minutes, convinced that whatever animal she was ogling this time was, "The coolest thing I've ever seen!" I didn't blame her, the Dubai Aquarium is unbelievably cool.

"So, what made you decide to bring me here?"

I tried not to smile, "My parents brought me here all the time growing up. It's one of my favourite places."

"Do you bring your *'work recruits'* here often?" She used air quotes to emphasise her sarcastic tone.

"No. I've never brought anyone here actually," I tried to keep my tone cool and controlled but failed a little. I could tell by her somewhat awed expression that some of the warmth had seeped in and cleared away the distance.

"Well, thank you. It's been a pretty decent day so far."

The trace of a grin danced around her rose tinted lips and I couldn't restrain the bubble of warmth in my chest. "The day isn't over quite yet."

After about an hour of oohing and aahing at thousands of fish we left the aquarium and began our trip toward the next spot.

•   •   •

Kiara

I think I'm falling in love with Dubai faster than I thought. I can't help but imagine a life for myself here. I love London with all my heart but I'm starting to wonder if I could live here. A fresh start. Downtown Dubai is like nothing I've seen before. It feels like London, New York and Los Angeles all combined into one beautiful, well-lit package without the mob of bodies and fear of being lightly trampled. I probably would have continued walking down that street forever. Or at least until my legs gave out. Palm trees were tucked neatly in the ground at equal intervals and wrapped around in lights that hung off the tips of their long leaves. There were also large camels and reindeer at every few hundred feet, adorned with even more lights. The mall looked down upon the pathways, covered in bright billboards and people glittered the roadway on either side. There were hundreds of restaurants and cafes overlooking the skyline.

"So, tell me. What made you decide to suddenly up and come to Dubai?"

A question right where it hurts. Of course, he doesn't know that. Does he?

I tried to play it off coolly but I was panicking internally about how to respond. I shrugged my shoulders in an attempt to look normal, "I needed a bit of a change. My Dad said he needed someone to supervise the Dubai office for a couple of weeks so I thought it might be good if I could come and help out."

The vein in his jaw ticked slightly, throwing me a little off kilter. *What's his problem?*

His mask dropped for a second, like he wanted to genuinely speak his mind but the walls went back up as quickly as they came down. "I guess everyone needs a change sometimes."

I laughed a somewhat bitter laugh, "Yeah, I guess so."

"I might be venturing out a little too far outside your comfort zone here, but I'm guessing you have hobbies? Or is being an absolute pain in the arse just one of your main character traits." And just like that, the arrogant arse is back.

I shot him my most withering glare, but it didn't make him recoil quite like I hoped it would. Instead, he broke out into a microscopic grin. I swear it must be painful for the man to smile considering how sparing he is with them.

"I have hobbies. Lots of them actually. Do you have any? Or is being an arrogant arse taking up all your time?"

He stifled a scoff, "No, it comes naturally to me actually."

I stood there slightly shocked with mild laughter and slightly speechless. Yes, he's an arrogant arse, but he *is* self-aware.

We continued walking in silence. The air hung heavy with discomfort. I would've rather not stayed to finish dinner together but my empty stomach wanted different things.

"Here we are. Mezze House."

We got a table for two outside facing the Burj Khalifa. A light show was being played across the entire building and it made the whole city brighter. I could feel a burst of warmth in my chest just watching it. I took another photo to post to my Instagram. I captioned it: Favorite city. I don't know what this city's doing to me, but whatever it is, it's working.

Dinner was incredible. Everything was fresh and absolutely delicious. We ate our food mostly in silence with a couple, "Could you pass me that?" and a few "This is amazing,"'s to pass the time. I was ecstatic when we got ready to leave. I had my driver pick up the car from DIFC this morning so it would be waiting back at the house when I arrived home. Instead of getting Kabir to drop me, I decided to cab it. At that point, I was ready to walk home if it meant I could avoid spending more time with him.

"Thanks for today. It was…nice."

"You're welcome. Goodnight."

I waved and scurried off to where my pink taxi was waiting for me. Another incredible thing about Dubai: there are female taxi drivers! Pink taxis are so cool, and for someone like me—who rarely cabs it home at night—it makes the whole cab experience feel so much safer.

By the time I reached home, I was battered. I got ready for bed as efficiently as possible and entered the sheets. I opened my messages to update my family and finish up a couple other work formalities. At the top of the list was the one message I completely forgot about: Jai. My stomach sank a little at the [3 new messages] indicator under his name. I'd let it slip from my mind yesterday and I was supposed to open it eventually. I took a deep breath.

You can do this. It's not that bad. Nothing he says will fix this, besides, you're fine on your own. You had a life before him and you will most certainly have one after.

13:01
Hey
How are you? It's been a couple days and I've heard nothing from you. Even Dhruv won't tell me anything. Everyone's been icing me out. Just talk to me Kiara, at least let me know that you're okay.
I didn't want it to end this way. Us to end this way. I miss you. A lot. I miss you a lot. Like everyday. I miss us grabbing coffee together in the mornings. I miss you during meetings. I miss you at our favorite restaurants. I miss you watching TV on my couch. I miss watching you read books. I miss us arguing. I miss you. Please talk to me.

The stitches felt like they were coming a little bit undone inside me. A silent tear slipped down my cheek and I tried not to break down. I thought it would be easier. I thought it would be easier to read the message and feel nothing. To keep the stitches on that hole intact, because I'd worked so hard to stitch it up in the first place. I wanted to be numb. To not have to feel like anything was hurting me. To feel like I didn't have a heart to shatter in the first place. But I did. And he'd shattered it. Not once, but twice. I felt pathetic more than anything. I felt stupid for feeling like this. For being hopeless. And helpless. And broken. Yes, I had a life before him, and yes, I will have one after but I wanted to live the rest of it with him. That was the whole point of it all. I didn't want to be alone again. To feel lost when I'd finally begun to find myself. I wanted to be sure that it would always be us against the world. That I didn't have to brave everything on my own anymore.

I guess I was wrong. Totally and utterly, wrong.

.   .   .

Kabir

God, why are you so stupid? Why do you say things like that?

I think I'm slowly beginning to understand why the entire world hates me. I'd hate me too. I can't believe I called her a pain in the arse. I barely even know her. I'm so stupid.

I buried myself in my sheets and continued contemplating.

At least tomorrow's the first day of a new week. A fresh start. An incredibly painful fresh start considering that she'll be practically on top of my head the entire day, but a fresh start nonetheless. I just need to survive a couple days of this and then hopefully she'll be on her way—and out of mine.

Chapter 5

Kiara

Nighthawk

noun

1. a recurring thought that only seems to strike you late at night

· · ·

There's something about being at work that feels like I'm in my happy place. Especially after last night. This is all I need right now. I just want to be buried in work. Like quick sand. I want to be trapped in an endless pit of work where feelings and emotions and marriage and ex-fiancés and weird work colleagues and obligations don't exist.

I put on a pair of charcoal grey cigarette trousers, a plain black top and grabbed my purse and laptop. I left the house pretty quickly. I wanted to be there as early as possible so that the working could start and the feeling could stop. I parked my car in the garage and began my trek to the coffee shop in the office building. After all the crying and wallowing that went on last night I desperately needed a little pick-me-up. Or a lot of pick-me-up actually.

I felt instantly better as the first drop of liquid caffeine hit my lips. I drank my coffee in peace for a bit, tearing through a couple more chapters of the book I was reading. I swallowed the last few drops of my latte by the time I'd reached the office. I took a deep breath and walked straight to Kabir's office. I didn't bother to knock, because while that would be common courtesy, he doesn't deserve my decency. Especially not after calling me a 'pain in the arse' yesterday. I'll show him just how much of a pain I can be.

"Good morning," he said without bothering to look up at me. God, he just makes me want to punch him in the face. I think workplace bylaws would frown upon that though so I'll restrain myself. For now, at least.

His frustration was still visible though. I could see the vein in his jaw tick again. His giveaway.

"Look up at me when you talk to me," my voice was a spear of ice. As Taylor Swift says, 'Darling I'm a nightmare dressed like a daydream.'

He looked up from his laptop and I could see the vein in his jaw tick again as he pursed his lips in a thin line, "How may I help you?"

"I think introductions are in order, don't you?" I smiled while making innocent puppy-dog eyes.

"Your staff needs to know who they report to for the next couple of weeks." *'Cause it sure as hell isn't you.*

I know how these types of guys work. What they're thinking when they're thinking it. They were both my friends and my foes my entire life. The industry that I work in isn't exactly very female friendly. It's cutthroat. Very few of us survive it. Then again, I'm not exactly one of the many.

I know that I punctured his inflated ego the first time we met and I can see the air escaping it quicker and quicker with each second we spend in this office together.

"Then let's give the people what they want," I could hear the exasperation in his voice even with his practised way of hiding it.

"Need."

"Sorry?"

"Need. You're giving them what they *need*," I added simply, a smile still stretched across my lips.

We walked out of his office leaving as much space as possible between us. As if a few feet of space would help with the growing frustration between us.

"Can I have everyone's attention please?"

The whole office gathered around us.

"I'd like to introduce Kiara Shah, CFO of Shah Enterprises. She'll be…She'll be *here* for the next few weeks." God, can he not even say one nice thing about me?

"You all report to her for the time being," he bit out the last sentence as if a gun was being held above his head. I mean technically it was standing three feet away from him.

I looked out at the crowd and smiled, "I'm looking forward to working with you all. The door to my office is always open."

He opened his mouth to dismiss everyone when I quickly shot out, "You're all dismissed." He shot me a dagger-heavy glare but kept his lips pursed in a polite smile. *So this is how it's going to go. Two can play at that game.*

I strode to my office in a quick and graceful motion, making a show of propping open my door so that people could come in at any time. He followed me like a hawk, watching every step with his eagle eyes and then disappearing into his own office. That was when I took a breath. Finally.

Two out of four walls of my office were made of glass and overlooked downtown Dubai. The views rivalled the views of my London office and I couldn't help but wonder if this one was better. I sat down at my desk and started sifting through the mountain of emails I'd ignored for the past two days. By the time I looked up from my laptop again it was dark outside.

I'd forgotten to eat, stretch my legs, basically do anything that made me even remotely human. I checked the time on my phone: 8:47 PM. God, had I really been here that long? I got up from my desk to take a walk around the office. It was empty. Everyone had left. Except for Kabir. I could still see a blue computer light shining in his room but I tried to walk past quickly so he wouldn't notice me.

"You're still here?" His voice seemed tired and incredulous, jarring from the cool, calculated mask he usually adopts.

I backtracked slowly, making sure to contort my face just enough to make him uncomfortable, "It would seem so."

He fixed his mask quickly and nodded. I continued walking but a slightly sick feeling plagued my insides. I walked to the coffee place downstairs and grabbed another cup of coffee.

I should probably head home. Then again, I didn't want to have to think about anything other than work. I'd managed to stay numb and clueless for twelve hours and I wanted it to stay that way. Even just for a little while longer. I don't want to have to think about everything.

I trudged back to my office and sat down, spinning my chair in the direction of the windows so I could take in the views as I sipped on my coffee. As much as I desperately wanted to go home, it was also the last place I wanted to be. Jai and I had been together since I was practically a child. Fresh out of college. I'd never experienced being completely alone. I lived at my own house and he lived at his, but we spent most nights together until I was just about ready to fall asleep, then he'd head back to his place. Something about the idea of freedom and living alone didn't quite sit right with me. Especially after I was looking forward to getting married and settling down with someone I wanted to spend the rest of my life with. It still feels like a hallucination sometimes. The breakup *and* the relationship. Being here has made me wonder if being on my own for a bit won't be so bad. Thinking about the breakup makes me physically sick though. I still can't believe that he called off the engagement because of a job promotion. A job promotion that he was fully aware we were both being considered for. I guess he never thought I was talented enough. Hell, I never thought I'd get it either.

I guess life works out in weird ways sometimes.

Knock. Knock. Knock.

"Hey, am I interrupting something?" He leaned against the door frame of my office, making all the muscles under his shirt flex ever so slightly.

Stop looking. I thought you hated him.

I straightened my back quickly, "No—no. Come on in."

"You sure? Seems like you were pretty deep in thought," he smirked a little, like he thought he'd finally figured me out. How cocky.

"I'm fine. What's up?"

"I ordered a pizza earlier. You want some?"

"Is this a ploy to apologise?" I made a coy face to make that vein in his jaw tick even more.

"I don't do apologies."

"My mistake."

"Come if you want some. Don't if you don't. I don't care." He turned and walked right out of my office.

I smiled a little to myself. The thought of making him frustrated makes me a little more satisfied than I'd care to admit. Although I desperately would've enjoyed completely ignoring his olive branch, I heaved myself off my chair and slipped out the door. He was sitting in his office, one hand typing furiously and the other shoving pizza into his mouth. He'd put on a pair of thin wire-framed glasses which somehow made his face look even sharper than usual.

And more attractive.

I sat down on the chair opposite his and grabbed a slice of pizza. He waited a good minute or two before turning his computer screen off and pulling the glasses off his face. He continued to shove pizza into his oesophagus like I didn't exist but I could tell that my presence made him uncomfortable.

Score! 2-1 Kiara.

I ate my pizza slowly and deliberately just to piss him off further. I tried to stop a smile from pushing its way across my lips but my efforts were futile, "Is there a reason you're smiling like that?"

His face was contorted to show his irritation.

3-1.

My smile doubled in size, "No. Jealous? I'm not sure that your face is capable of doing the same."

The vein in his jaw ticked, he really must be more careful with his tells. He let out a sort of growling sound before going back to forcing pizza down his throat. I picked up a second slice just as he went to grab another one and our hands fused. It felt like a warm spark shot down my arm and I pulled away immediately. He grabbed a slice and pushed it towards me before picking up another himself. I grabbed the slice and excused myself, "Thanks for the pizza."

"You say thanks an awful lot for someone who isn't obligated to."

"Manners aren't an obligation. Some people are actually nice of their own free will, you know. I'll see you tomorrow."

.   .   .

"AHHHHHHHHHHHHHHHHHHHHHHHHH!"
Imagine the most high pitched scream you've ever heard.
Now add a heart-attack and morning voice. That was how I
was woken up this morning.

I think I'm scarred forever. Waking up will never be
the same again.

"What the f*$% is wrong with you two? How the
hell did you even get in? I'm going to kill you both." I woke
up to find Amara and Nick standing over me. They blast
confetti cannons when I opened my eyes, leading to the
heart-attack of my life. I swear if I was twenty years older
that would've been it. They would be murderers.

"Good morning to you too!" Amara was far too
cheery for 8 o'clock in the morning. It was pissing me off.
I'm not a morning person as it is, blasting confetti cannons
and scaring me to death definitely doesn't help with my
relationship with waking up early. I don't think I'll ever
recover.

"Hi there sleepy head," they both climbed onto my
bed to hug me.

"Mngggggggg," I pulled the sheets over my head and
tried to escape.

"Time to get up, come on, you have a long day ahead
of you." Nick pulled me off the bed micro-aggressively. If
that's even a word. I couldn't think at all. All I wanted was
more sleep.

I trudged into the bathroom and made myself look
semi-presentable before going downstairs to the kitchen
where they were waiting for me. Amara handed me a cup of

coffee, "Here, maybe this'll make you like me a little more." She smiled a watery smile and I could tell she was holding back a series of laughs.

"Thank you," I breathed in the scalding caffeine and instantly felt better. Coffee solves everything. Well, maybe not everything. But most things. I'll stick with that.

I sat down at the marble island opposite Nick and Amara. "So, how goes the honeymoon-ing?"

They both smiled at each other and it made my stomach sink a little. "It's amazing. We spent the majority of the last week just eating and sleeping and swimming. Well, he did the majority of the sleeping," Amara elbowed Nick in the stomach.

"Hey! That was so not my fault." They remind me of little kids sometimes. I guess they aren't anymore. None of us are. I can't say growing up is my favourite. Definitely not.

I sipped on my coffee and left them to go get dressed. As much as I love the two of them, and love them together, it's the last thing I want to see right now. That was me ten days ago. Everything feels different right now though. Some days I forget that my heart was broken, other days it's so unbelievably evident. I guess I just don't want it to define me.

•   •   •

Kabir

So it turns out that my parents decided to go full speed on Operation Get Kabir Married. It's getting exhausting. They're showing me girls every other second and expecting me to fall in love over some meaningless marriage profile, no doubt created by the desperate parents of some single girl that has just barely passed out of college. It's become my entire life. I've been spending nights at the office for the past few days. I mean entire nights. I fall asleep at the office and wake up at the office. It's become a nightmare. I'm worried one of my staff is going to find me passed out at my desk some day in the same clothes as the day before. I'm worried *Kiara's* going to find me like that.

So you do care what she thinks.

It's not like I don't want to get married. I do. I just don't like people in general. I can't even be nice to my boss. How the hell am I supposed to tolerate a woman living in my house for the rest of my life? I'm not made for the whole family lifestyle. I'm not made to be a bachelor either. I'm just—cliché as this may be—a lone wolf. I stay away from the human species and it stays away from me. That's just how I like it.

The only people I'm able to tolerate are my parents. And I'm avoiding even them right now. I've been working hours and hours overtime to avoid the dating profile marathon that ensues when I go home. I don't even live with them anymore but I manage to find them at my house. Every. Single. Night. So I've resorted to sleeping at the office. It's easier this way. Quicker. Maybe not more painless. But quicker.

I looped the last loop of my tie in the mirror in my office and left to go get a cup of coffee from the coffee shop downstairs. I grabbed an espresso and decided to wander around the grocery store for a bit. I hadn't been eating much either. This whole not-staying-at-home-multiple-days-a-week was starting to take its toll. I secured a cart and went to town. The grocery shopping experience was like a blind rage. I got protein bars, sparkling waters, quinoa chips and dozens of chocolate protein drinks. By the time I was back at the elevators on my way to the office, Kiara had arrived.

"Morning!"

"Well, you seem awfully chipper." I kept my tone as deadpan as possible.

"I guess I am," she smiled to herself, "My cousin and his wife are in town."

"Exciting," I replied with mock enthusiasm, to which she replied by rolling her eyes viciously.

Ding.

We both entered the lift and reached over to press the button. My hand fused with hers and I could feel a rush of electricity running down my fingertips. She pulled her hand away and allowed me to press the button.

"Don't tell me all those snacks are for you."

"Okay, I won't."

She gaped at me, "You're kidding. Is it even possible for a human being to eat that much?"

I kept looking straight ahead, "Yes."

An awkward silence filled the air until BANG! We were both suddenly on the elevator floor in a tangled heap.

"Are you okay?"

"Yes. Are you?"

"I will be once you get off of me."

She blushed and pushed herself off from my chest. I'd broken her fall when the lift dropped. We both stood up and tried the elevator doors. They were stuck together. Badly. I wasn't sure if we were at a point where we'd be able to get out even if I could unjam the doors.

"And, we're stuck."

"Thank you for that announcement. See if you can get any cell service, we need to be out of here as soon as humanly possible," God, she thinks she can boss me around. How self-righteous. I got on the phone with the building manager while she anxiously paced around the two-foot cube of space between us. "We're not getting out of here for a while. They've already assessed the damage but they said it'll be a good few hours before they can get us out."

She groaned and slumped against the corner of the elevator. I slid into the opposite corner, leaving as much space between us as I could in that tiny death-trap of an elevator. I don't know what'll kill me first: the elevator or Kiara. I'm willing to bet it'll be Kiara.

I opened up a protein bar and started eating.

"How can you eat at a time like this?" Disgust contorted her delicate features.

"No point in being stuck *and* hungry."

Agreement flashed across her face before she went back to eyeing me angrily. I chewed extra loudly to make her fidget with her hair even more. It's her tell. Whenever she gets frustrated she twists her hair into ribbons or braids it or plays with it. It's annoying as hell.

No, it's attractive as hell.

"You want some?" I waved the packet of quinoa chips in front of her face. She growled at me before grabbing the packet from my hands like a feral animal.

Once she opened the packet and started eating she was much calmer. *Thank God, maybe the elevator will have a chance to kill me first today.*

"So, how should we pass the time?"

I shrugged, "No idea. Why don't you decide?"

"Look, it's yet another man pushing responsibility onto a woman instead. How shocking." Her voice was deadpan but I could hear some sort of emotion lying beneath it all. Like buried pain.

God, why are women so difficult?

"You clearly have some sort of deep rooted issue that I'm not sure I want to get into right now." I wanted to slap myself a little at that moment. I rarely feel bad for speaking my mind but telling my boss she has a "deep-rooted issue" is definitely not the way to go about this extremely uncomfortable conversation. Especially considering how…fragile she seems. I felt even worse when I saw her eyes glaze over.

Kiara

Stop crying. No-one can see you weak.

I don't know why but my eyes were filled with tears again. I thought I was done crying. I thought this city was healing me. It was, but I guess some parts have to break a little more before they can truly be fixed. I sometimes wonder if that's why I fell in love with Jai. I was quite broken when I met him. It was like finding a small ray of sunshine amidst an endless sky of angry clouds. I was in my senior year of college when he entered my life. I was going through a phase of burnout and depression. I didn't tell anyone though. To everyone else I was perfectly happy.

I don't think it's that he saw through any of that. It's more like he helped me remember who I was beyond the layers of pressure and anger and sadness that had been pent up for so long. I was having trouble finding myself and he sort of did that for me. Maybe that's why I feel so lost now.

Then again, was I only in love with him because of that? Did I fall in love with the first thing that made me feel like myself? I might be overthinking this.

"Kiara? Earth to Kiara? Hello?" God the words coming out of his mouth were more than deja vu, it felt like I was in a trance, or a terrible dream. Either way, he's capable of making me feel both.

"I think it's best if you just leave me alone."

"Look, I'm sorry. I'm not exactly great with people."

I stayed silent and avoided looking in his direction. He turned over to look at me, opened his mouth to say something then slumped back onto the elevator wall.

He's not wrong, he really is terrible with people.

Internal dilemma. Why are people so complicated? I don't want to talk to him. I don't want to be mad at him, mostly because I'm not. It's really not his fault. He may be a terrible person, but none of this is his fault. Jai is the one that broke my heart.

I closed the few feet between us and pretended to grab a bottle of sparkling water from the grocery bag.

"I'm sorry. Really."

I waved my hand, "It's fine."

"So, what are we doing to pass the time?"

I grabbed my laptop from my bag, "*I* will be working."

He smiled to himself as I opened up my laptop. *Why is he looking at me like that?* I started opening up my emails and documents but nothing would load. A 'Couldn't load. Please refresh.' button plagued all of my screens.

"So, what *are* we doing to pass the time?"

"You want to spend time with me that badly, huh?"

He shrugged his shoulders and shook his head but I could see a faint smile playing on his lips.

"Let's just talk." I sighed quietly, leaning against the elevator wall.

"Okay, fine, what do you want to talk about?" His voice was deadpan but he was slumped against the wall and I could hear him breathing. In and out. I tried to focus on that instead.

"Anything."

"Tell me about Jai."

I slowly turned to face him. I couldn't help the shock that contorted my face, *how does he know?*

"Who?"

"Your fiance, or I guess now it's ex-fiance."

I took a deep breath, "There's nothing to tell. Things didn't work out. That's just how it is. Can we talk about something else now?"

"You know, it isn't healthy to just skip past these conversations like they don't exist. But if it makes you *that* uncomfortable, we can talk about something else."

"It *is* healthy to move on from this topic because I've had this conversation. Ten different times. I don't *need* to talk about it anymore."

The vein in his jaw darkened slightly, "I guess I'll talk about my own life then."

I listened intently as he started. "Like I said, I was born and brought up here. My parents moved here when there was almost nothing. They've seen the whole country progress to where it is now. They've been here for about thirty years. According to them, there were only a few buildings and centres when they came. Well, *that* and a whole lot of desert. I've travelled the entire world with them, yet every time I come back, I feel at home. I've never felt at home anywhere else. The UAE truly is the best place to live. I wouldn't be happy anywhere else. That's part of why I chose to come back a couple years ago." He was talking slowly and quietly, like giving out even basic information about himself scared him.

"What about your love life then? Do you have a special someone?" I teased, nudging his shoulder slightly before sinking back onto the wall.

He looked at the ground and gritted out, "No."

"Shocking."

"Right? I mean who wouldn't want a piece of this." He gestured to his body but kept his voice completely flat. *Insecure. He seems insecure. Interesting.*

"I could probably name ten people,"

"I could too," his laugh rumbled through the elevator. It was sweet and coarse and played on the edges of my ears.

I wouldn't mind hearing more of it.

He pushed his head onto the back of the elevator, "I haven't been in a serious relationship. At least not for a while. I got caught up with school and work and life, I guess. Turns out I don't really like people either. Not the most dateable person overall. So, I decided to just push everyone away. That way, I don't hurt anyone, and they don't hurt me. Easy. Quick and painless."

Quick and painless. I always say quick and painless. Maybe we're more alike than I thought.

He laughed for a second and then became quiet again. I smiled, "What was that little laugh all about?"

He smiled, a tired but sweet smile, "I haven't been home in three days."

My jaw practically fell to the floor, "Three DAYS?! Why?"

"My parents are back on Operation Get Kabir Married *again*—yes, I know how stupid that sounds. Ever since I got the promotion to head of the Dubai office, they're determined that it's the right time to get me married. I mean they tried before that too but I made the excuse that I needed to focus on my career for a little while before I could jump into starting a family. They bombard my house every night with the excuse of family dinners, only for the three of us— four if my little Sister, Ayla, tags along to watch me suffer— to end up on the couch sorting through hundreds and hundreds of Shaadi.com profiles. It's become a nightmare." He looked at me wide-eyed as if he couldn't believe that he'd just admitted that to me. I tried not to burst into laughter, especially after seeing how solemn his face remained throughout the explanation.

Keep your composure. No laughing. Think sad thoughts.

I burst into laughter anyway, water droplets stinging my eyes and cramps tormenting my internal organs. He stared at me in amusement before bursting into laughter himself. The sound rumbled through my insides again. *What is he doing to me?*

"Shaadi.com profiles, that really is hilarious," I paused to let out another wheezy laugh and wipe my eyes, "Have you really not found anyone yet?" I felt my cheeks getting heated at my own interest. There's no reason for me to be interested. I'm barely over my last relationship as it is.

He shook his head and stared straight ahead, going the tiniest bit red and flushed on his cheeks.

"Do you know what you're looking for, at least?"

He continued to stare straight ahead, as if looking me in the eyes would unlock something he wanted to keep closed. "Not really."

I practically exploded from where I was sitting, "How can you not know?" It's not exactly fair for me to assume that he'd be ready to get married or even know what he wants in a partner when I'm one of the few people that is ready to get married, settle down, have kids and a career at the ripe age of twenty-four.

"I never gave it much thought. It's not like it's very high on my list of priorities."

.   .   .

Kabir

I mean she isn't wrong, why don't I know? I've been alive for an entire twenty-six years. By now most people have dated around, got into relationships and even gotten engaged. I mean, the prime example of all this is sitting right next to me.

"I never gave it much thought. It's not like it's very high on my list of priorities." A complete lie. I might be emotion averse but pretty much everyone has thought about it at some point. Surprising, I know, but even heartless monsters like me feel lonely sometimes.

"Fine, think about it now then. What do you think you'd want?"

I sat there for a minute, fidgeting with my hands and trying to decide whether or not I should lay the cards out onto the table. What would I want? I tried to make a mental list:

- Needs to be extremely intelligent

- Self-sufficient

- Career oriented

- An interesting person (at least one of us has to be remotely entertaining)

- Extroverted introvert

- Has to love food

- Should want to have a family?

Hell, I don't even know if I want to have a family. I'd never want to spring that onto a woman, especially because she'd have to do all the work. I'm heartless, not immoral.

"I guess she'd have to be intelligent—" Kiara nodded, listening intently, "She'd have to be self-sufficient. Therefore, if I break her heart she'd never become dependent or lose her ability to survive."

Kiara gave me an incredulous look before saying, "The surety in the likelihood of you breaking her heart is concerning but I guess there's some logic to that," she pushed me to proceed.

"She'd have to be very career oriented so it's never a problem if I'm caught up with work because she'd get it. Balance. She has to be interesting and have hobbies—" I would've included the part about me being the most uninteresting human on the planet but I didn't want Kiara to have any more leverage against me.

"She also has to love food." Kiara crinkled her nose in confusion as I finished my last sentence.

"What?"

"It's nothing, it's nothing," she shook it off quickly.

"You clearly have something to say so get it out with."

"You say that you want your S.O. to love food, but you looked at me as if I was crazy every time I ate and enjoyed my food."

I tried to stop the laugh that was clawing its way through my lungs. I wasn't looking at her as if she was crazy, I was trying to cover up my amusement. And clearly I didn't do a very good job of it.

"I wasn't looking at you as if you were crazy. I found it—for lack of a better word—cute, that you were enjoying your food so much." I kept my voice as dispassionate as possible, knowing that even a note of emotion would go straight to her head.

"Interesting, so you *do* think I'm cute." her voice echoed through the elevator.

I shrugged my shoulders, "Whatever makes you happy." She smiled bigger.

"Anyway, you were saying."

"I wasn't. I think that's all I'm looking for."

.   .   .

After talking for hours—and consuming an entire grocery trip's worth of snacks—we fell asleep. She was asleep on my shoulder when I woke up, breathing slowly. In and out. In and out. In and out. I tried not to move at all. I didn't want to wake her.

Ding.

I got a text from the building manager saying that he was finally going to be able to get the elevator doors opened. I nudged Kiara softly, pushing on her arms to try and wake her. She just stirred slightly and shifted further on top of me, "Mngggghh, five more minutes."

"Kiara? They're going to get the elevator doors open. I think you might wanna wake up for this." I nudged her slowly and she opened her eyes, looking straight up at me. She jumped up, like she'd forgotten where she was. Who she was with.

She rubbed her eyes vigorously and settled back into her seat, "Hi."

•   •   •

Kiara

I didn't realise how many hours it'd been of us arguing and talking until the elevator doors finally opened some time close to seven o'clock in the evening. The sun had already fallen down and it felt like I was stepping off a plane with a deluded sense of time. We were asleep on the floor when they finally opened the elevator doors. I woke up on top of Kabir. At least he didn't wake me up aggressively. He was quite sweet actually, giving me time to get up before the doors opened.

I walked out of the elevator on wobbly legs before he called out to me again, "Kiara, wait."

I turned back around to find Kabir trying to catch up, "What's up?"

He caught up and started walking in step next to me, "You wanna grab dinner?" I felt somehow taken aback by his proposition for a dinner date. The hours we'd spent together in the elevator felt like an out of body experience. I didn't understand how we'd gotten along for so long in such a small space. "Sure, I could use some dinner."

We left the office and walked down downtown to TimeOut Market. I ordered pizza and we sat down at a table with high chairs. We ate in silence but it was a comfortable sort of silence, the kind of silence that you'd have with a friend.

Or maybe someone more.

.   .   .

Chapter 6
Kabir

I had to go home that night. There really was nowhere to hide anymore. Nowhere to go. I had to go home eventually. I prayed that my parents would decide not to bombard my home that night. I didn't have an option either way, I desperately needed a shower longer than ten minutes and I wanted to not live in a suit for the rest of my life. As stupid as I feel for even thinking it, all I wanted was a hot shower, my pyjamas and to sleep on my own pillow for a night. Instead, I had my parents, a hot plate of roti sabzi and my dog, Dude, passed out on the couch. Not bad, but not a whole lot better either. I was grateful for the sabzi, not so much for my Mother and Father sitting at the dining table with their reading glasses teetering on the tips of their noses, faces illuminated by the blue-ish laptop light.

"So, beta, I found a few more girls on Shaadi.com for you to look at," My Mother was squinting at the laptop while simultaneously turning it towards my Father so he could have a look too. I continued shoving roti and aloo ki sabzi down my throat, mumbling a few "Mhmm"'s to keep her happy.

"Kabir! You're not even looking. God, I'm telling you, he's never going to find a good girl," she looked up at the ceiling as if she was genuinely complaining about her emotionally unavailable son to God. I didn't blame her.

"Yes, yes I'm looking. Show me the next one."

She flipped past to the profile of the next girl. Either I was losing my mind or they were all starting to look the same. I wouldn't be surprised if it was a bit of both.

"She's perfect!" This was probably the third time my Mother had uttered those words that night, practically every girl was *'perfect'*.

"Look Kabir, she's an engineer, she went to a school in the US, she's perfect. She's pretty too. I scrolled through her profile, slowly getting curious about all these profiles myself. My eyes immediately floated to the 'Interests' section of the webpage. Under the tab 'Alia Agarwal's Interests' I could read the words I'd read on practically every other profile: cooking, cleaning, raising a family. Those three things were beginning to become my least favourite attributes in a person. I shrugged and handed the laptop back to my Mother, "I don't know about her."

My Mother just shook her head and launched into yet another long-winded explanation about how I was never going to find a wife if I didn't try. After about the third minute of her lecture I had zoned out and was starting to see shapes in the raita. A bunny rabbit riding a volcano? Or no, maybe it's a dog eating ice-cream. Either way, I was slowly losing my mind. Slowly but surely. Then, my Mother gasped. Loudly.

"I know what this is about! I know exactly what this is about!" She bounced on the spot vigorously, shaking my Father's arm as she whipped her glasses off her nose and perched them on top of her head.

My Father just looked at her incredulously, sighed and then proceeded to scroll through the Shaadi.com profiles.

"You're dating someone, aren't you Sid?" I tried to hide the absolute shock and epiphany that crossed my features with those six words. I don't know what evil monster possessed me, but I said "Yes." My Father looked up from the laptop, his face clad in the first emotive expression he'd shown all day: shock. He took his glasses off his nose slowly and set them on the table before breaking out into a grin. He was smiling from ear to ear, and it looked as if the corners of his lips were going to rip from the effort.

I took a breath to think about the seriousness of what I'd just done. I just said I have a *girlfriend. Me.* A *girlfriend.* A girl who's not just a friend. I don't have one of those. God only knows where I'm going to find one. On the plus side though, I don't have to endure these Shaadi.com profile nights anymore. I can come home, shower, eat and sleep in peace. My life will be back to normal. Well as normal as it will be once my Mother starts asking about my non-existent girlfriend. I just screwed myself over big-time, didn't I? Well, I guess I'm screwed then.

"You're crazy Bir. Your father and I have been looking at girls for weeks for you and here you're sitting with a girlfriend. Unbelievable," the frustration quickly set in. "Well, what's her name then?"

I could feel my gut churning but I kept a straight face, "Kiara."

"You're dating Kiara Shah?!"

"Yes."

From there, the night was a series of a million questions to which I answered with 'yes' and 'no' and 'I don't know'.

All I know is, *I'm screwed.*

.   .   .

I could hardly wake up this morning. I don't know if it's because the adrenaline had finally caught up with me and I was no longer forcing myself to run on fumes or if it was because of the extremely elaborate and highly stupid lie I told last night. I'm willing to bet that it's a healthy combination of both. Mr. Shah is having a black tie gala to celebrate the opening of the Dubai office tonight and all I can think about is how Kiara's going to strangle me when she finds out what I did. That is if I can even get her to agree to be in a fake relationship with me.

I don't usually drink coffee but it feels like a coffee sort of morning. Kiara and I were the first ones at work, as usual. The silence is starting to become more comfortable between us. The air doesn't feel as thick and toxic. The tension is still palpable and could easily be cut by a knife, but I can't feel any hostility in the atmosphere. I waltzed straight into her office, knocking on her open door in a gesture of peace.

Knock. Knock.

"Guess who finally learned how to knock," she remarked, not bothering to look up from the stack of papers plaguing her desk.

I leant against the wooden doorframe, "Turns out that manners aren't an obligation after all."

She looked up and gave me a small smile, "Stop quoting me."

I closed the door behind me and I could feel my heart sink to my stomach as I mentally prepared myself for what I was about to say.

Kiara gave me an almost panicked look, "Wh–why are you closing the door?"

"We need to talk."

"What did you do?" Her voice had the strongest condescension, like a Mother scolding her child.

"Nothing." Well, that's sort of a lie.

"Spill. Now."

"I went home last night—"

"Congratulations," her voice was deadpan as she returned to the stack of papers in front of her. She placed a neon yellow highlighter in her mouth while highlighting through documents with a bright pink highlighter, scribbling neat notes in the margins.

"So, I went home last night, and lo and behold, my parents were there." She mumbled an 'Mhm' and continued dyeing the entire page with an assortment of pink and yellow, switching the highlighter out in her mouth as she moved along. "They began talking to me about marriage and were showing me Shaadi.com profiles and I was seeing shapes in my sabzi and then well, I-sort-of-told-them-that-you-and-I-are-dating."

She looked up from her highlighting with furrowed brows, "Could you repeat the last part? I couldn't really understand what you said."

"Well, I-sort-of-told-my-parents-that-you-and-I-are-dating but obviously it's nothing serious and you don't have to be worried about it." I mumbled through the important bit as quickly as possible.

"Kabir, for the love of God, out with it."

My stomach churned slightly, I'd never been nervous before. I'm supposed to be a cold heartless monster. I've been told I'm one of the most ruthless bosses that my staff have ever had and yet this feisty five foot two woman makes me nervous. What has my life come to?

I took a deep breath and leaned on the side of her desk, looking out towards downtown.

"I told my parents that you and I are dating."

I thought for a moment that all my courage had come back. That the cool, calm and calculated Kabir had made a return. That no woman had the ability to make me nervous. That was all before she uttered her next three words,

"You did what?!"

She jumped up from her desk and went straight for my neck, scattering the papers and highlighters all over the floor. She managed to jump onto my back, one hand wrapped tightly around my neck and the other hitting me on my shoulders.

"I'm going to kill you! You're a psycho crazed heartless crazy monster! You told your parents that we're dating without even telling me! Are you mental? You know what, I think you actually are mental. Remind me to admit you to a mental institution" I let her go on like that for about seven and a half more minutes before she was panting and wheezing loudly, slumped over my shoulder, arms still hanging around my neck.

"Well, if you'd let me get a word in," she proceeded to wheeze in my face in response, "What I was going to ask you, is if you would mind pretending to be my girlfriend, just for the next two months. All I'm asking for is sixty days. Sixty days, sixty nights and we never have to do this again."

She continued panting and replied between broken breaths, "What makes you think I'm even staying for the next two months?"

I set her down on the sofa and handed her a water bottle, "I don't think you're leaving any time soon Kiara."

"Why would you think that?"

I smiled, "Because I see that look in your eyes whenever we go out. The slight twinkle, the excitement at every little thing. You've fallen in love with the city. Whether you want to admit it or not."

She thought about it for a minute, like she was doing every cost-benefit analysis possible in her head. I stared at the floor while I waited, studying the patterns in the marble to see if I could find any shapes.

"Fine."

I looked straight into her eyes and didn't even bother to hide the pure shock on my features.

"I'll do it."

Kiara

Litost

noun

1. the hurtful feeling experienced when you unexpectedly see the person responsible for your heartbreak

.   .   .

There has to be scientific evidence that states that heartbroken people do stupid things. There just has to be. I spent the better half of my day printing, highlighting and reprinting documents. I couldn't focus. As much as I hated to admit it, the whole gala thing had me rattled. Kabir and I were going to make our public debut with little to no practice on this whole fake-dating thing. Only God knows why I agreed to it in the first place but I'm hoping it has something to do with the fact that I'm trying to move on from Jai.

Or maybe it has something to do with the fact that you're hopelessly attracted to him.

We've come up with a sort of idea of what to say and how to behave but the whole idea still makes me feel sick to my stomach. Like a whole swarm of butterflies swimming around my abdomen.

Let's be honest. They're the good kind of butterflies.

So, I did what any rational person would do and ditched work for the mall. It's not like I was getting anything done anyway. I stopped by Kabir's office before leaving.

Knock. Knock.

"Hey, I'm heading out. Last minute shopping to do for the gala tonight. I'll see you there?"

He looked down at his desk—which was relatively bare and far tamer than mine—before saying, "Need company?"

I thought about it for a minute. As much as I can't stand him—*liar*—I wouldn't mind having someone to help carry around the shopping bags. I tossed him my keys, "You can drive."

"What is it with you and your obsession with being—what's the term you used—oh yes, '*passenger princess*'? Most moronic thing I've ever heard, by the way."

I scowled, "It's a totally normal concept, thank you very much."

. . .

The gala was perfect, exactly the way my Dad had envisioned it. I walked around, mingling and thanking people for their congratulations on my new role as CFO. What I wasn't expecting was to see my ex-fiance and Sanya together. I don't mean like he's her date for one night. I mean like, they're holding hands and he has his hand on the small of her back and he's fetching her drinks kind of together. I could feel my food coming up at the sight of it all. I got quite busy making the rounds that I lost Kabir. I was more than surprised when I felt a pair of arms wrap tightly around my waist from behind. I tried not to look surprised, "Is this your way of trying to spook me? Because I can assure you, it's not going to work in the slightest."

He bent his head down toward my ear and whispered, his breath hot on my skin, "Based on the way you froze in my touch, I'd say it's working pretty damn well."

"Careful, you're behaving like you don't hate me."

I felt a smile creep across his face, "Rest assured, I definitely still do, love."

Jai and Sanya walked over to us and I expected Kabir to straighten up or back off, but he kept his arms firmly around my waist, forcing me to melt into him.

"Kiara, long time no see!" Sanya hugged me with the biggest plasticky smile on her face. I hugged her back before Kabir pulled me back into his hold. I felt suffocated, but less by Kabir and more so by the ambush of Jai and Sanya. No-one had warned me he'd be here. Worse than that, no-one had warned me that he'd be here with *her*.

"Sanya, lovely to see you as always," I could feel myself gritting out the words but I took a deep breath and continued to smile. She scanned me from head-to-toe, looking for any weaknesses I'm sure. I did the same. My eyes tracked down her figure and stopped at her hand. I could feel my saliva catch in my throat, closing it up. Her left ring finger was bound by a ring. A diamond ring. An engagement ring.

I felt like I couldn't breathe. Like there was a weight on my lungs, crushing and heaving. Making each breath impossible. I was physically hyperventilating and I needed no-one else to know.

You need to breathe. Slow down and breathe. Just breathe Kiara. No-one can see you like this.

I felt Kabir's warm arms creep around my waist again, like a silent plea to calm down. He bent down and whispered, his lip just brushing against the peak of my ear, "You can do this. Just breathe." He drew lazy circles on my back, the motion guiding me towards slower and deeper breaths.

Jai looked over, "Kiara, long time no see." He smiled wearily, pretending to be happy for everyone else. I could tell though. I knew him well enough for that.

Not long enough.

"Long time indeed."

Kabir held out his wrist, keeping one arm firmly wrapped around some facet of my being.

If I'd know he'd be this possessive I'd never have agreed.

Jai shook his hand, "Jai Anand."

"Kabir Kapoor."

Jai smiled at me, "Nice to meet you." Kabir smiled a sly smile and I could feel the butterflies take flight in my stomach. I felt sick.

No, you felt alive.

"The pleasure is all mine."

I thought the tension in the air was going to suffocate somebody before Dhruv walked over, allowing it to dissipate completely. He hugged, "Kabir! It's been forever, man." It took him a whole minute before he noticed our arrangement and I watched his face fall. "I guess it really has been a while. Uhm—anyway, I need to talk to you two slightly urgently," he turned to Jai and Sanya, "If you'll excuse us."

We walked past the sea of people to some dark corner before my brother practically exploded, "I'm going to refrain from physical violence for now. But get your hands the hell off my Sister before my patience runs out." Kabir held firmly on and I could feel my entire body get one million degrees hotter. I tried to wriggle my way out of his grip but he wouldn't let go. Dhruv turned towards me, "Explain. Now. Preferably before I punch him."

I turned to Kabir, "I'm going to tell him the truth. He needs to know. Besides, I can't lie to him." Kabir nodded, keeping his jaw tightly clenched. I could see his vein tick again, a stark blue against his fair complexion. I turned back towards my brother, who was eyeing up Kabir with a murderous look in his eyes. "We're—in a false relationship. We're just fake dating to get through the next few events and to get his parents off his back. I–I'm-not-even-sure-why-I-agreed-to-it-but-I'm-here-now." I took a deep breath and smiled a watery smile.

"You're crazy Kiara. You're actually mental sometimes." He chuckled lightly, "But you need to keep this up for as long as possible. Jai's having his destination wedding here—to Sanya."

I felt my blood run hot. Like fire bleeding through my veins.

He winced, "I'm sorry we didn't tell you sooner. You were just doing so well and I didn't want to put you back ten steps. Mom and Dad agreed too."

I tried not to lunge at my brother, "When is the wedding?"

Dhruv didn't meet my eyes.

"When is the bloody wedding, Dhruv?" I barely managed to grit my words out as my eyes welled up with teardrops, threatening to barrel down my face.

"It's in two months."

"When were you planning on telling me?"

"Tonight. After the party."

I linked my arm with Kabir's and began to walk us back, "We'll talk about this later." He turned to me as we left my brother behind, stopping in his tracks. "Kiara," he pulled me backwards, "I think we should talk about it. It's not healthy for you to keep it bottled up."

I sighed, "There's nothing to talk about."

He pulled my chin up with the tip of his finger, forcing my eyes to meet his, "We're going to talk about it at some point. Whether you want to, or not."

I growled softly and slipped my arm back through his outstretched one. He chuckled and led us back into the room.

"Kiara!" This night was going to be long. Very, very long. Definitely not quick. And definitely not painless.

"Hi, Pinky Auntie. So lovely to see you." I don't understand how this woman is at every party. She's followed me to a different country. I swear I'll never be able to get rid of her.

Kabir held firmly by my side, no doubt sensing the frustration plaguing my tone. My battery was starting to drain.

He cut in, "Hi, I'm Kabir." He kissed the back of Pinky Auntie's hand and for a moment I wondered if I was losing my mind.

She blushed and giggled, "So handsome this one."

I moved back into him and mumbled just loud enough so he could hear, "Where did that come from?" I continued to smile a fake smile at Pinky Auntie, saying the words through closed teeth.

He replied the same way, a plastic smile still plastered across his jaw, "I never said I couldn't pretend."

My focus quickly shifted from my pretend boyfriend to Pinky Auntie, "Did you hear about Jai's engagement? He bounced back so quickly. She comes from a great family too." Pinky Auntie was having a great time rubbing it in and I was just standing there taking it.

He put his arms around my torso and pulled me into his bubble of warmth, "I think Kiara bounced back pretty quickly too."

After that Pinky Auntie's face went through a million different emotions. She looked shocked one minute, confused the next and ended it all with a devilish smirk on her face. I felt that sickening feeling in my stomach again.

They're called butterflies. And they feel incredible.

"Well, I'll leave you two alone. Don't have too much fun!" I swear that woman drives me insane. I gave her a forced chuckle and small wave goodbye.

"So, you seem to like her." I could hear a laugh bubbling in his throat as I eyed him bitterly. I walked myself to the bar and he followed. Like a puppy.

"Can I get a coke, light ice? Thanks."

"A *coke*? Must be serious," he was trying to lighten the mood and honestly, it was sort of working. I didn't know he had it in him to be the happy one.

"I would love to just ditch all this and go home right now," I sighed and sipped on my coke.

He shrugged, "I actually kind of like these things."

"How can you enjoy all this? The greeting and meeting and explaining. I can't take any more. I'm done."

He grabbed one of my hands and set my coke down on the bar, "Breathe. It doesn't have to be difficult if you don't make it difficult. Let's dance." He pulled me through the crowd despite my pleas and I could feel myself growing more and more nervous. I felt sparks fire up the side of my hip as he placed one hand there. The other was in mine on the other side of my body, making us look like a well constructed human teapot. The music wasn't particularly terrible, though I'd always been a stickler for a good love song. We swayed gently with the beat and I refused to look in his eyes. I didn't want this to get any more intimate than it was. My skin heating at his touch was already a cause for concern and besides, we're supposed to *hate* each other. I don't plan on changing that any time soon.

"My eyes are up here, love."

"I'm well aware of that," I could feel my cheeks redden.

"So what you're saying is that you'd much prefer to imagine my abs under my suit?"

I wasn't paying attention to where I was holding my gaze and it happened to be right about where his abdominal muscles would be. That is, if he even has any.

"I'm not sure you'd even have any for me to imagine."

He smirked and bent down so our faces were just inches away from one another, "I'm full of surprises." His breath was hot against the apples of cheeks and I could feel goosebumps break out across my face.

He slowly pulled back up, as if he knew just how nervous he made me and was somehow satisfied with the fact.

"God, don't look so smug."

He settled back into his usual resting depressed face but I could see the ghost of a smile on his lips, "I'm not smug." He was smiling entirely at this point and honestly, I hated it.

He was smiling entirely at this point and honestly, I loved it.

God, I can't stand him.

Liar.

I looked up into his eyes, giving him exactly what he wanted.

Liar. You wanted to look into his eyes. You wanted to see him smile.

"Finally."

He held my eye contact, burning his sepia eyes into my own, like he was branding me. I didn't break either, and it felt like a game. That neither of us wanted to lose. So we stood there, moving in a neat rhythm of steps and staring into each other's eyes like our lives depended on it. I liked the competition though, the idea that I could beat him.

"Let's have a little wager,"

He raised his brows in amusement, "I'm intrigued, go on."

I rolled my eyes, "Whoever breaks eye contact first loses. If I win, you owe me one."

"And if I win, you owe *me* one."

We kept moving in our neat cube of steps, passing other couples without once breaking the line of contact running between us.

"I think you're going to break first." I bet he said it just to fire me up.

"And why do you think that?"

"Because I know you. You think you can't stand me, but spoiler alert: you can. You deny that my touch makes you nervous, although I'm very well aware that it does. Your tendency to blush betrays you."

I blushed again.

"You also think that you're going to win this bet, which I assure you, you will most definitely not. You know how I know?"

"How?"

Suddenly, he dipped me. His arm held firmly under the arch of my back and I leaned into his touch. It felt like the world slowed for a moment, maybe even came to a stop. I broke eye contact for a split second, but only long enough to squeeze my eyelids shut tightly in shock. Maybe he didn't notice.

He definitely noticed.

"Because of *that*," he'd pulled me back up and was almost beaming with satisfaction. He wrapped both his arms around me as the song ended, hugging me tightly. I tried not to feel any comfort at his touch. The feeling of his warm hands against my back, his chin sitting on top of my head, I tried not to feel any of it.

I felt it all.

•   •   •

Kabir

God, the feeling of her hand in mine, of my hands on her hips, I tried not to feel any of it. I tried and tried. But God, it felt so good. I didn't know it would feel so good. I didn't know making her blush or making goosebumps break out across her skin would feel this good. I didn't know I was capable of feeling human emotion like this.

"You cheated," Kiara had the biggest frown on her face, and she was giving me the evil eye from a distance. I guess she *is* a sore loser after all.

"There were never any rules to begin with." I've always been a ~~rule breaker~~. Or maybe the correct term is rule bender.

"God, you infuriate me sometimes."

I tried to swallow the chuckle that was hurtling through my throat, "I know, love."

"Stop looking at me like that."

I nearly choked on my own breath, and straightened up quickly, "I didn't realise I was looking in the first place."

Liar.

She just sighed and put her head against my chest in frustration. "I'd do anything to kill you right now." Instead, I pulled her into yet another hug. Less for the show of it all and more for my own selfish tendencies.

"I know you would."

.   .   .

"You have to drive me home. I can't drive in these," she pointed aggressively to her ridiculous shoes.

"There's always the option of public transportation." Even with Dubai's incredible public transportation infrastructure I wouldn't have actually denied her a ride. I just have to make sure that I play my role as the soulless colleague.

She tossed me the keys, "Just shut up and drive me."

I mock gasped and unlocked the car, "A woman who knows what she wants. I like that."

She settled into the car and put her knees under her chin in a foetal position, resting her head on the car seat. It didn't take very long before she dozed off. I could hear her breathing softly.

In and out. In and out. In and out.

I watched as downtown became suburbs and roads became plush with greenery, still listening to her faint wheezy breaths as she slept in the seat next to me.

I didn't want to wake her when we reached her house, so I unlocked the car and carried her out—ridiculous shoes and all. And somehow, I didn't hate doing it. I didn't hate driving her home. I didn't hate dancing with her. I didn't hate listening to her sleep in the seat next to me. I didn't hate any of it.

I carried her up the stairs and into her room onto the bed.

God she looks beautiful.

"Kiara?"

She didn't answer, didn't even stir.

"Love?" This time I shook her lightly, just gently pressing her shoulder blade to wake her. She responded by pushing one arm out in the direction of my face, nearly poking my eye out with her long nails, "Mmmnng."

She remained asleep.

"God, you're going to kill me one day." I walked myself to her bathroom and started looking for makeup removing wipes. I don't know what compelled me to sit there and try to remove her makeup but it felt like a good decision in the moment. I returned from the bathroom and tried to wake her one last time, "Kiara?"

She still didn't stir.

"Hell," was all I whispered before I began slowly removing the makeup from her face. I gently brushed the wipes across her soft skin until they came up clean. After that, I tucked her into her bed, carefully securing her under the warm sheets. I stopped for a moment to look at her face. She looked so peaceful.

And beautiful.

Then I quietly padded out of the room.

Maybe I don't hate her all that much after all.

Chapter 7

Kabir

Kairosclerosis

noun

1. the moment you realize that you're currently happy

.   .   .

Ding.

1 new message from The Devil.

Messages from the devil are always good. Who doesn't love Lucifer, right? I opened my Contacts app and scrolled to Kiara's contact.

I should change it, I thought.

My finger hovered over the 'First Name' section and I deleted 'The Devil', though I'd enjoyed seeing it pop up on my screen every time she messaged me. I typed in, 'Kiara' and deleted it again. I retyped 'The Devil' and closed Contacts. Just didn't feel right.

12:41
Morning
Morning
I hate saying this
Intriguing, do go on
God you're an arse
I just wanted to say thanks for last night
I'm assuming you were the one who tucked me into bed and removed my makeup
If not, I really need to get some security cameras installed
Not confirming or denying anything
Though I strongly suggest the security cameras, especially for makeup removing criminals
Why can't you take appreciation like a normal person?

12:41
Why can't you take appreciation like a normal person?
Who said I was normal?
Right, my mistake
I'll see you at work
Kabir. It's a Saturday.
Damn
Don't you have a life? Go do something with it
What're you doing with yours then?
That's a good question
Ummm...
Hold please
...
Yeah I've got nothing
I'll meet you at your house in an hour

12:43
Kabir. It's a Saturday.
Damn
Don't you have a life? Go do something with it
What're you doing with yours then?
That's a good question
Ummm...
Hold please
...
Yeah I've got nothing
I'll meet you at your house in an hour
Don't worry about the dress code, I'm bringing you clothes
KABIR?!
You can't just invite yourself to my place like that

I closed my messages. Ding. Ding. Ding. Ding. Ding.

5 new messages from The Devil.

I think opening those is against my best interest. I cleared the notifications and called my sister, Ayla, to ask a favour.

"Hey."

"You're calling awfully early in the morning. What do you want?" Surprisingly enough Ayla is the more cynical one out of the two of us.

"Can't I just call my Sister?" I sugar-coated my voice.

"No. *You* can't. Cut to the chase please, I have to get ready for brunch with the girls." With the way she was talking I could tell she was stretching her face to put on mascara.

"Can I borrow a set of workout clothes? They're for—a friend." I could feel my blood run hot, like flames had suddenly erupted in my veins.

"Does this friend happen to be your new *girlfriend*?" Suddenly, she was interested. She paused and I could almost picture the look on her face on the other side of the phone: eyebrows raised, breathing slowed, mascara waiting to be applied only inches away from her eyes.

"I'll be over to pick them up in ten," I hung up the phone.

.   .   .

Kiara

Men think they're so high and mighty. They can do whatever they want, whenever they want. Not today Kabir Kapoor. Not today.

Ding dong. Ding dong.

I stood right outside my front door, listening to Kabir ringing the doorbell. He'd rung it about three times and I'd already made him wait outside for about ten minutes.

Ding dong.

"Kiara! I know you can hear me."

I just laughed, "Still not sure how that's supposed to convince me to open the door."

"For the love of God Kiara Shah, open the damn door."

I waited till my stopwatch hit exactly twelve minutes and I opened the door to find Kabir Kapoor standing at my door. He was clothed in a way that can really only be described as odd. I wasn't sure what occasion he was dressed for. He was in a hoodie and sweatpants which either meant that we were doing something that required us to get messy, or we were going to do nothing at all. The latter option definitely sounds more appealing to me.

He held a mysterious bag outstretched towards me and growled, "Here. Go change."

I just stood there, with a—hopefully—defiant expression on my face, "No."

"Go. Change. Now."

"No."

"Kiara, for the love of—you know what, I'm not doing this right now," he threw me over his shoulder and started walking up the stairs. I pounded his back with my fists, hitting as hard as I could. Spoiler alert: didn't work.

"Put me down. Now."

"No," was all he said before he walked into my room and put me down on the bed. He threw the clothes down next to me and barked, "Change. Now."

He closed my bedroom door on his way out, leaving me trapped inside. I tried to open the door but I think he was holding the handle closed and as much as I hate to admit it, I'm no match for his strength. I'm blaming it on his sheer size, not the muscles.

It's definitely the muscles.

"Let me out!"

"Not until you're changed."

"How exactly are you going to test that theory?"

"I have my ways."

"God, they better not be weird."

"Get your mind out of the gutter, love."

I opened the bag to find a sports bra, crop top and cycling shorts, "I AM NOT GOING TO THE GYM KABIR!"

"That was one of my ways."

"I'm being one hundred percent serious. I will not set foot in a gym today." I don't know what it is but I don't believe in working out. Or I just don't like it. It's definitely one of those.

I've never been to the gym before.

"Fine, you don't have to set foot in a gym. Just get changed."

I struggled my way through putting on the sports bra that was definitely a little too small for my upper half and slipped on the crop top and shorts to go with it. I knocked on the door, "Let me out, I'm done."

. . .

Kabir

"Let me out, I'm changed."

I probably should've checked the workout clothes my Sister packed for Kiara. I thought I could trust her to pack something sensible. Something that wouldn't force me to have to peel my eyes away from my fake girlfriend.

I opened the door and there she was, pulling at the shorts and the t-shirt as if it would magically make them bigger.

"What're you staring at?"

I straightened up quickly, "I—Uh—Urm—Let's go."

I walked into her kitchen and started sifting through the cupboards for a water bottle. She walked in behind me and sat on top of the kitchen counter, "What are you looking for?"

"A water bottle."

"Why would I need a water bottle if we're not going to the gym?"

"I'd assume you need water in general, like, to live. Or no wait, I forgot that you're the devil incarnate." I rolled my eyes at her, "I wouldn't mind a little help with the water bottle." She rolled her eyes at me and huffed, getting up to help me.

She slid into the space in front of me between the counter and my body. I felt her back press into my chest as she leaned back to open the door. My chest immediately heated to one-hundred degrees where her back touched it, like she'd branded me as her own.

She grabbed my palm and cupped it around the bottle, "Here." I felt my hand turn molten under her touch. God, what is she doing to me?

Maybe she makes you just as nervous as you make her.

I filled her bottle and we were about to enter the car when I tossed her the keys and said, "Why don't you drive today? I wanna see what's so special about this whole *'passenger princess'* thing."

She laughed, "You? Passenger princess? Please, that's the funniest thing I've ever heard."

"Who said men couldn't be princesses too?" I kept my voice entirely deadpan as I opened the car door for myself.

·   ·   ·

Kiara

Driving with no knowledge of your destination is a surprisingly terrifying experience. It's not like I had much of a choice anyway, Kabir wanted to experience passenger princess life. "Which way do I turn now?"

"You have Waze on your phone. Use it."

"Just tell me where to turn, arsehole." God, he infuriates me ~~sometimes~~. Correction: he infuriates me all the time.

"Take the next right."

"Thank you. Now was that so hard?"

"Yes, it was actually," he slumped into his seat to prove his point and I could see a phantom smile on his lips. He'd taken his hoodie off and I could see purplish veins running through his muscled arms. The tshirt he was wearing was so tight I felt like I couldn't breathe, for him. I tried to keep my focus on the road and not on his muscles that were teasing my eyes through the folds of his black tee.

So you do find him attractive. Eyes on the road, Kiara.

I mock frowned, "Very funny."

He kept his voice flat, "I didn't realise I was joking."

I shot a death stare in his direction and he smiled gently. I hate his smile.

No, you love his smile.

"Keep your eyes on the road, love."

"Don't call me love."

"Why not?"

My breath hitched in my throat as I opened my mouth to speak. I didn't have a valid reason as to why he couldn't call me love, "I—don't know, actually." And if I'm being honest, it's attractive as hell. Which is exactly why I don't want him to use it. We're supposed to hate each other. Everything else disobeys the basic laws of nature.

Maybe you don't have to hate him all that much.

I pulled into the parking lot and we left the car. The sign outside said Fitness First and I knew then what I'd been roped into. "I'm not setting foot in there. I'm going home."

He jogged over to the other side of the car as I got back into the driver's seat. He grabbed arms and pulled me out gently, cupping his hand over the arch of the car door to protect my head. "Like I said, you don't have to set foot in there." He pulled me away from the car, stole the keys from my hand and locked the car.

"Kabir, I'm serious. I'm not walking in there."

"I know you're serious, love. Which is why you don't have to."

"What is it with you and the word loooooveee—" I never got to finish my sentence because he hoisted me into his arms. I was forced to wrap my arms around his neck. He held me like I was going to crumble, like I was made of porcelain. He was holding me right up against his body, as if distance was difficult for him. Like it was hard to be away from me. I could feel my pulse quickening as he walked us toward the gym.

"What? No plea to put you down this time?"

I shook my head, cheeks flushing at the consistent contact between his body and mine. He taunted me with a quiet laugh and adjusted his hands under my knees and back.

He put me down, "I told you you wouldn't have to set foot in a gym, love."

"Creative."

We passed by the receptionist and Kabir shot her a wink. She stared at us in amusement and I just mumbled a "Hi" from the confines of his arms. I could feel my face flaming crimson.

.   .   .

He shrugged and shot me a cocky smile, "I guess I'm just that good." He handed me a pair of boxing gloves and mumbled, "Hold these." Kabir grabbed a roll of tape and started wrapping my hands. I felt my hand retreat under his touch when he started wrapping my palm, "Relax."

I blushed, "I'm relaxed."

"No, love. You're not." He continued wrapping the tape around my wrist gently but tightly.

"What makes you say that?"

He closed the wrap on my right hand and started on my left, gripping my wrist. He traced a lazy line along the size of my hand and up my arm, making me shiver. I could feel goosebumps break out everywhere on my body but I tried to keep my feet planted firmly to the ground.

He lifted my chin so I'd be looking directly into his eyes, "That."

I shook my wrist in his direction and cleared my throat, "Just—Um–Just keep wrapping. Uh—please." He smiled and mumbled something under his breath, but I couldn't hear it.

.   .   .

Kabir

"God, you're going to kill me one day." I whispered it to myself just loud enough that I could hear myself. I don't know what she does to me.

. . .

Kiara

"Hit me."

"What?"

"Hit me." He opened his arms in a gesture of violence, "You need to get some of that pent up aggression out. Hit me." I stared down at my gloved hands and back at Kabir. He was smiling tentatively, like he genuinely wanted to help me. I closed the few feet between us and held my gloved hands in a fighting stance in front of my face. He didn't have to tell me twice. I know my way around physical violence. My Dad forced Dhruv and I to take Taekwondo when we were younger, and we weren't allowed to stop until we were black belts. I hated it, but I can always win in a fight. Verbal or physical.

I pushed one fist out in the direction of his shoulder and punched. Hard. He stumbled backward slightly and looked at me with widened eyes.

"I know my way around a sparring ring."

He smirked, like a light bulb went off in his head, "Then let's make this a fair fight."

A few minutes later, Kabir was donned in a pair of gloves identical to mine and we both took fighting stances across from each other. I closed the distance between us again and we sparred. I threw blows everywhere but his face and kept my other wrist in front of my own to protect myself. He was good, I'll admit, but no match for me. Within minutes, I had him pinned to the floor, wrists pressed to the floor with me hovering on top of him, "I win."

It felt good to be in control. To have the upper hand.

He was breathing hard but grinned at me, "You sure about that?"

He surprised me by flipping over our position, pinning my wrists to the floor and hovering over me. He bent so close to my face I could feel his heartbeat. My blood raced at the feeling of his body so close to mine, of the feeling on his hands pinned on top of my own. "Clever, but not clever enough."

I flipped us both back over the mat again, so he was on the bottom and I was above him. He smiled lazily at me, "I surrender." I stood up and held out a hand to help pull him up. He grabbed it and pulled me down onto him, so we were a tangle of limbs and heartbeats. He started laughing and I couldn't help but do the same. We laid there laughing for a while.

And for a moment, maybe I forgot that we were supposed to hate each other.

.   .   .

Kabir

My heart wouldn't stop beating at the speed of light and I willed it to slow down. I didn't want her to know how nervous she makes me. The way she makes my heart race, my rationality take a rain check and my limbs go weak. We were a mess of limbs but damn it felt good. She didn't even pull away when I pulled her onto me. We just stayed there, fused together, laughing.

She smiled at me and I swear I felt something crack in my chest.

It's the ice thawing around your heart, dumbass.

"So, what now?"

I hadn't actually thought that far ahead. What was I even supposed to say? "Whatever you want."

She raised a brow in mock surprise, "No grand plan?"

I shook my head in surrender and helped her disentangle herself from me. "Let's go back to my place." Her eyes widened and I quickly corrected myself, "Just to order food and watch a movie. On *separate* couches."

We spent the entire ride on the way to my house laughing and talking. I drove this time. I'd had enough of the passenger princess life. Though I guess I understand what she loves about it so much. Every time she'd laugh I could feel that crack in my chest.

Like something was healing, not breaking.

•   •   •

We got out of the lift and I opened the front door. It was still light out but the sun was slowly starting to set on the horizon. I could see the clouds below us, like wafting spirits passing through the breeze-filled eve air.

She rushed to the windows in my living room, "This is incredible." She whispered it, almost like it was a secret. Like this view was a secret, something only she and I could see. I stood behind her, looking out of the window myself. The sky was painted in hues of valencia, rose, cherry and plum.

"It is pretty amazing." I tend to forget it myself sometimes. I forget how incredible this place is. How beautiful. My eyes drifted back to Kiara, who was still taking in the eventide sky.

She's even more beautiful.

I walked over to my kitchen and started pulling out ingredients. I grabbed a box of macaroni, cheese, milk and the spice box. My Mother had given me that spice box when I first moved in. It feels like a rite of passage to have one of these. Especially since she's the one who taught me how to cook. My Mother is eccentric in that manner. While most Mothers expect their sons to be mischievous and play sports, mine expected me to learn to cook, clean and excel at academics.

Kiara followed me into the kitchen with the most perplexed expressions, "What are you doing?"

I held up the box of pasta in my hand, "Playing dress-up. What does it look like I'm doing?" I grabbed a pan from the cupboard and started the kettle.

She took a seat at the marble counter and watched, "You can cook?"

I turned around, leaning on the edge of the countertop while I waited for the pasta water to boil, "No. I just enjoy attempting to boil pasta for recreational purposes." I tried to wipe it clean but I could feel a smile work its way onto my lips.

She rested her chin in the palms of her hands, elbows propped up on the counter, "You are just full of surprises."

I gestured to the pot of pasta boiling on the stove, "You wanna help?"

"Sure. But I'll warn you, I'm much more of a baker."

I set another pan on the stove, adding in butter then flour and mixing those together. I waited for it to boil and added the milk. The pasta finished boiling but I couldn't take it off the stove because I couldn't stop stirring the sauce, "Drain the pasta and run it under cold water before it gets overcooked."

She gave me a small salute and I swear I felt my knees buckle. She really is going to ruin my life.

She drained the past and left it in a glass bowl, leaning on the counter next to me while I stirred the sauce, "Who taught you to cook?"

"My Mum. She believed that boys and girls should all have the same skills. Which means that my Sister had to become a sports pro and I spent my time in the kitchen."

She smiled, "That's so sweet. I took up baking in high school. It almost became a coping mechanism to deal with school stress and exam pressure. There was always a lot of pressure to get into a top school and perform really well, so I needed something to keep me grounded."

"Do you bake anymore?"

"Not really. I never leave enough time to." Something about her eyes didn't sit right with me. She was smiling but it was a crestfallen sort of smile. Like one that appears on your face when thinking about a distant memory, something fond but it makes you ache thinking about it at the same time. Wistful.

"Are we going to talk about it?"

"About what?" I could see the mist slowly clear away from her eyes as her thoughts returned to the present.

"About whatever you were thinking about when you zoned out just then."

She sighed, taking a deep breath, "Jai and I used to bake. Together. Most weekends." Her face returned to some state of numbness. It was like all the life was somehow sucked out of her whenever she talked about him.

"What even happened between the two of you?" She hesitated as I finished my question. I sighed and added, "We don't have to talk about it if you don't want to. I don't think it's healthy to keep it bottled up like this anymore though. Yes, sparring is a good way to let off some steam, but that's all it's good for: letting off steam. You need to actually talk about it if you ever want to rid yourself of the weight."

She thought about it for a moment, like she was actually wondering if talking about it would help. I continued stirring the sauce. The sound of the spoon scraping the pan filled the silence.

"Jai and I dated for four years. We got engaged about six months ago and we were supposed to get married next spring. Jai and I both knew going into all this that we were being considered for the same promotion: CFO. We'd always worked together so it never felt like it would be a problem. I was so in love with him, and I'd like to think that he felt the same way too. I was appointed as CFO close to two months after our engagement. Nothing seemed wrong to me. He even threw me a huge party to celebrate. We'd started planning our wedding and everything. Then, at my cousin Nick's wedding, he broke it off. Said that he couldn't be with someone that was in a higher position of power than him. I think it was less his doing and more his parent's doing. Still, those words hurt. I guess I just never expected it."

I took the pan off the heat and set it aside, listening intently. She took a deep breath, so deep it made me question if she'd been breathing the entire time we'd been together. So deep I wondered if oxygen had ever properly permeated her lungs before. I could feel my muscles tense up as my brain processed what my heart was telling my body to do. I pulled her into a hug, resting my head on top of hers, breathing in her floral perfume. She didn't even resist. She just wrapped her arms loosely around my waist, burying her head in my chest.

"I've never said the whole thing out loud before," she whispered it into my clothes so softly I could just barely make out her words. Like saying it a decibel louder would make it more real. Scarier.

I kissed the top of her forehead before pulling her face closer to me so her eyes would meet mine, "Thank you."

"Why would you thank me?" She was still talking quietly, processing everything she'd just admitted to me.

"I just felt like it was time."

•   •   •

She fell asleep on my couch that night, in the middle of watching some old episodes of Suits. We started off on separate couches—like I'd promised—but ended up with her sleeping on my arm anyway. I didn't have the heart to wake her. To send her home. Away from me.

I took a minute to study her face. And I mean really study it. Suits was still playing in the background and I could barely hear Harvey cursing at Mike over the sound of my thundering pulse. Her porcelain doll face looked almost breakable. Like one wrong move and she'd shatter to pieces. That's how she felt sometimes too. I was always worried I'd make one wrong move and the whole thing would come tumbling apart.

I scooped her into my arms and walked to my bedroom. I undid the sheets with my free palm and set her down gently in the middle of the bed. She adjusted herself on a pillow, still fast asleep, and I tucked her under the sheets.

You're giving her your bed? Since when do you suddenly have a heart?

I grabbed a blanket from the cupboard in my room and retreated to the sofa. *I guess the sofa it is tonight for me.*

You're screwed Kabir. And I couldn't be happier about it.

•   •   •

Kiara

I woke up at Kabir's apartment the next morning. In his bed. It was odd to say the least.

I must've fallen asleep or something. Hopefully.

When I walked outside he was sitting at the kitchen counter drinking coffee.

"Morning."

"Hey," he smiled at me, "Morning."

His smile. Oh his smile.

I poured myself a cup of coffee and stood opposite him behind the counter.

"So, I have something to tell you."

I felt a churning sensation in my gut, "Mhmm."

"You have to meet my family today."

I nearly spewed my coffee everywhere. "I have to *what*?!"

He winced, "You have to meet my family today?" He smiled at me again, probably trying to soften the blow.

It's working.

I shouldn't have been as shocked as I was though. It was part of our fake dating agreement. What's the point in having a fake girlfriend to bypass your parents trying to get you engaged if they never actually get to meet her?

I took a deep breath, "What time?"

"In an hour."

"I. Am. Going. To. Kill. You. Kabir, please explain to me why you didn't let me know yesterday. Or even woke me up sooner so I could get ready? I swear you're so thick sometimes." I grabbed my keys from his coffee table and made my way to the front door.

"Where are you going?"

I stuck my head through the other side of the door, "Home. Your fake girlfriend needs to keep up appearances."

He smiled.

I drove home as quickly as I possibly could and jumped in the shower. I wasn't sure what to wear to meet his parents. I hadn't done the whole *'meet the parents for the first time'* thing in a *while*. I pulled on a flowery mini dress and called it a day. The dress made me look like a girlfriend: innocent, feminine and easygoing. I didn't feel like one, but I guess it doesn't matter as long as I look like one. I grabbed a small purse and slung it over my shoulder before leaving the house. After that, I drove back to Kabir's apartment. We agreed that we'd go to lunch together from there, but our one hour was getting awfully close to ending. I called him from the car, putting my phone on CarPlay so I wouldn't have to use my phone. "Call Grumpy."

"Calling Grumpy," called out the female CarPlay voice.

I waited as a couple dials went off. Ring. Ring. Ring. Ring. Then he finally answered.

"Hey."

"So I know you said an hour, but it's almost one thirty. You sure you don't just wanna meet at the restaurant?"

"It's better if we're late. My parents are notorious for being a minimum of fifteen minutes late everywhere. Besides, on the rare occasion that they get there first and you get there after—before I do—would you be comfortable with braving them alone?"

I gulped, "On my way to yours."

He chuckled and it rumbled through the speaker phone, "See you in a bit, love."

God, what if I totally screw this up? What if they absolutely hate me? I hate this whole fake dating thing. I don't know how to be a girlfriend when I'm not a girlfriend. I don't know how to make myself comfortable around him, especially when I can hardly stand him anyway.

Lies.

I pulled up outside his building so he could get into the car. Honk. Honk. He looked up from his phone and started jogging toward me. He got into the car and we took off in the direction of the restaurant. Today's destination: Canary Club. I'd never been there before but Kabir said the food was to die for. And he hadn't disappointed me thus far.

.   .   .

Kabir

I thought I'd be more nervous to have my fake girlfriend meet my family, but I wasn't. *Maybe because sometimes it feels less fake and more real.*

We were going to Canary Club, which is where we always do Sunday brunch as a family. I was just excited to see my parents as me, not as some bachelor they're desperate to get married. We were seated at our usual table, waiting for my parents. Kiara was being awfully quiet, and fidgeting with her hair a lot. Twisting it in between her fingers in round loops. Over and over and over again. I took her free hand and squeezed it, "You okay?"

She smiled but it didn't meet her eyes, "Perfect. Why?"

I laughed at her outright lie, "Liar. You're fidgeting with your hair."

She stopped immediately, letting a loose strand fall to her shoulder, "So? Everyone fidgets with their hair sometimes."

"Yes, but for you it's different. It's one of your tells. It's how I know you get nervous. Or frustrated."

She smiled a hesitant smile and said, "How do you know that? No-one knows I fidget with my hair when I'm anxious." She whispered it, like it was a secret to be kept just between the two of us. I just shrugged and winked at her. I pay more attention to her than I'd like to admit.

Then, the Kapoor khandan* arrived. We both shot up from our seats, still holding hands. She looked down at our intertwined fingers then completely retreated her hand, face turning a cherry hue.

My Mother ignored me completely and went straight for Kiara, pulling her into a hug, "Kiara! We've heard so much about you. It's lovely to meet you, darling."

Kiara smiled and I could tell she wasn't nervous anymore, "It's lovely to meet you too Mrs. Kapoor. Kabir talks about you all the time."

Then my Mother suddenly seemed to remember her son, and she pulled me into a hug, "Hi beta." She whispered in my ear as she hugged me, "You never told us she was so beautiful." I felt the insides of my cheeks heat and I mumbled a short laugh before retreating to my seat.

My Dad shook hands with Kiara, "It's wonderful to meet you Kiara."

She shook his hand back, "The pleasure is mine, Mr. Kapoor."

My Sister pulled her into yet another hug, whispering something intelligible in Kiara's ear, making them both laugh before they took their seats.

.   .   .

Kiara

His Sister pulled me into a hug, whispering in my ear, "You've got him wrapped around your finger." We both laughed. I tried to ignore the butterflies that entered my stomach when I looked over at him. He was beaming at me.

.   .   .

Kabir

She took her spot next to me and I whispered as she sat down, "What was that all about?"

She smirked, "Nothing for you to worry about."

I felt butterflies empty their way into my stomach at the sight of her smirk. She is going to ruin my reputation as a heartless monster, isn't she?

"So, Kabir, how's work?" My Dad asked, studying the menu intently.

"Work is good. Hectic. We're pretty much up and running now, though." I looked over at Kiara who was smiling as I talked about our hard work. My Mother brushed our conversation away, willing it to end, "Enough about work. How are you enjoying Dubai, Kiara? Has Bir been good about showing you around?"

I was tempted to laugh. 'Showing her around' was how I got myself into this mess in the first place. I must've let out a small chuckle or something because Kiara elbowed me in the stomach. Hard. I ignored the sharp pain in my abdomen, which only seemed to amuse her more.

"I love Dubai. Some days I wonder if I can go back to London after experiencing this city. Ka—erm—Bir, has been great about showing me around. He took me everywhere the first couple days. And we explore new spots together every weekend." She looked in my direction, batting her eyelashes to really sell our story. I was still hung up on the part where she called me Bir. It was strange to hear my childhood nickname come out of her mouth.

But strange in the best way.

Ayla gestured between us, "So, how did this whole thing happen then?"

Kiara went very red and very quiet. She looked towards me in a silent plea to answer. I wasn't sure what to say myself but I knew that a half-arsed explanation would suffice. "We hung out a lot between work and me showing her around everyday. Eventually I worked up the guts to ask her out on a date, and the rest is history." We looked at each other and then around at everyone else. My parents were smiling and so was Ayla. Kiara and I looked back at each other and I could see the relief in her eyes.

Mission accomplished.

Chapter 8

Kabir

Xeno

noun

1. the smallest measurable unit of human connection

.   .   .

Ring. Ring. Ring.

Incoming call from The Devil.

I laugh pretty much every time I see her name come up on my phone. It's particularly dangerous when I'm in meetings and she sends me a text. I've almost burst out laughing on far too many occasions.

I answered, "Yes, love?"

Mock gagging sounds rumbled through the speakerphone in my car, "It's too early for this kind of behaviour Kabir, save it for the yacht."

Kiara and I are throwing a yacht party for Diwali. Together. As a *couple.*

"It's four-thirty, love."

"Still way too early."

"Are you almost ready? I'm on my way to pick you up."

She laughed and I could tell that she was going to enjoy torturing me, "I'm *definitely* almost ready. Don't you worry, Kabir." I love the way she says my name. The way the consonants rolls off her tongue.

"What's the game plan tonight?"

She sighed, "We just have to survive it, I guess."

I chuckled at the depressed state of her voice, "Try to sound at least a little excited, love."

"I am. I think. I'll see you in a few."

"See you in a few."

I got to her house and found her outside, on all fours, donned in a lehenga, with a lighter in one hand and a dia in the other. She looked up, "Hey!"

I whipped out my phone to take a picture and instead of retreating like I thought she would, she smiled, holding the lighter and dia like props. She stood up after I finished taking the photo, dusting off her lehenga.

My breath hitched in my throat.

God, she looks amazing.

She always looks amazing. But put her in a lehenga. My God, steals the breath right out of my lungs.

I walked toward her and she screamed, "Stop! Watch out for the rangoli. I spent an hour on that." She gestured to the rainbow powder sitting at the edge of the entrance to the house. She'd drawn a big, feathery peacock in the middle, surrounding it with colorful flowers and swirls.

"My bad, love. You need some help with the dia's?"

She nodded, handing me my own lighter so I could work on the rest of the dia's she'd laid on the entrance to her house. She bent back onto all fours, making her concentration face while she tried to light the rest of the candles.

.   .   .

Kiara

I love Diwali. It's the best time of the year. It's like my birthday, a wedding and Christmas all rolled into one. I don't think there'll ever be a better holiday. That is, if I can manage to light these damn dia's in time.

"Done. You need me to help you catch up there love?" He had the most smug expression on his face and all I could think about were vicious ways to wipe it off. I think slapping it off could be fun. Cruel, sure. But fun.

So would kissing it off.

My intrusive thoughts don't see the light of day very often.

I handed him my lighter and retreated into the house, "You can finish for me, *love.*"

He just shook his head and chuckled, lighting the candles while I went to get my bag. I walked back to my front door, leaning on the door frame while I watched him light the remaining dia's.

Damn, he looks good.

I hate admitting it, but Kabir looks pretty dang attractive in a kurta. It's quite terrible, really. Black kurtas always have me in a chokehold.

I think he outdoes everyone else, though.

What I'm trying to say is, I've seen better. I think. Maybe.

He hopped up once he'd lit the last one, placing the lighter on the table next to the door and holding out his arm for me, "Shall we, love?"

I took it, rolling my eyes and trying to suppress the smile that was forcing its way onto my features. He walked me to the car, bending down to help me get my lehenga inside. I couldn't help but feel a little nervous to have him so close to me. So in control. His hand just barely brushed against my calf when he pushed my skirt inside the car and I felt myself shiver.

God, ~~what is wrong with me~~? Correction: what is he doing to me?

I tried not to think about how nervous I was during the entire ride to the Dubai Marina. The idea of throwing a party with my significant other—who isn't actually my significant other—was making me feel surprisingly nauseous.

. . .

Kabir

She looked almost green when I looked back at her. Pretty close to the minty color of her lehenga. I tried to keep the conversation going but she was limiting her responses to single syllables.

"Kiara, are you okay?"

She nodded, still looking out at the skyline. I could tell she wasn't though. She tends to lie about her state of being. A lot.

"We're here."

I got out of the car and rushed to open the door for her from the other side.

"You are such a show off, I hope you know that." She was smiling now, and looking far less green than before.

"I might be a show-off, but at least I bring a smile to your pretty face."

She blushed and rolled her eyes simultaneously, "Save it for the boat, Kapoor."

We both got onto the boat where our guests were already waiting. The plan was to watch the sun set and then go wild at night.

"Showtime," I whispered into her ear, standing behind her, like the model couple we obviously are. She straightened up in front of me, smiling like her life depended on it.

. . .

We lost each other for nearly an hour, completely wrapped up in meeting our guests. I was breathless and exhausted by the time I found her again. I'd said 'Happy Diwali' so many times the words were starting to lose their meaning. She was having a conversation with Ajay Uncle—who seemed far more invested than she was. I approached them, taking a deep breath.

I held out my hand, "Ajay Uncle! So good to see you." I don't know where all the additional energy came from, but I guess saving my girl is important to me.

My girl? You're losing it, Kabir.

I carried a two minute conversation with Ajay Uncle before I pretended that the DJ was in dire need of assistance,

"I'm so sorry Uncle, I think the DJ needs our help. Please excuse us."

We both moved to the head of the boat, leaning against the railing to take a breath.

She hugged me, "Oh thank you! I could kiss you right now. Between him convincing me to invest in cryptocurrency and all the talk about my financial plans for the company, I was on the brink of losing my mind."

I'm pretty sure I stopped listening after she said, "I could kiss you right now."

I wish you would.

•   •   •

Kiara

"Let's dance."

He looked at me wide-eyed, probably remembering my hesitation the last time he asked me to dance.

I rolled my eyes, pulling his arm in the direction of the dancefloor, "I love dancing. You'll see."

He chuckled softly before moving in the direction of the dancefloor, "Oh will I now?"

I just shrugged my shoulders and smiled at him. The DJ was playing 'Pasoori' and everyone had made their way onto the floor.

Thank God. Now the fun can begin.

I put Kabir's hand on my shoulder, tugging him behind me as I danced my way onto the floor. Everyone was caught up in their own thing, drinking and singing and having a good time. That's the best thing about parties—no-one's paying attention to anyone, everyone's just having a good time. He stared at me with animated expressions as I danced. I screamed the lyrics at the top of my lungs, willing him to sing with me. He grabbed my hands and started dancing, sending me twirling and pulling me close to him. There probably wasn't even an inch of space between us, but I didn't care. I didn't want to think about anything except the music.

.   .   .

Kabir

She wrapped her chuni around my neck and continued to dance, shaking her head and hips wildly. I could barely take my eyes off her. It's like she's a different person when she dances. So wild and carefree. Nothing like the uptight girl who bottles all her feelings. Unfortunately, I don't have quite as much stamina as she does. I pulled myself off the dancefloor and over to the bar to grab a bottle of water.

"Hey, could I get a bottle of water please? Thanks."

Tap. Tap. Tap. I felt a hand on my shoulder.

"Water? Must be serious."

I turned around, "You're such a copycat, love."

She was visibly shaking, the wind was whipping around us. I took off my jacket and wrapped her in it.

"Thanks. But you didn't have to do that."

I rolled my eyes, "You were visibly shaking, Kiara. Learn to accept help."

She chuckled, raising her brows, "I could give you the same advice."

We just stood against the bar for a moment. And that was when the fireworks went off. Hundreds of them. Like stars bursting in the sky.

She wrapped an arm around my waist and I swear I felt firecrackers burst on my skin. I put my arm around her body, pulling her into me. Closer. We stayed like that, just watching the fireworks, neither one of us wanting to move. To end this. Whatever it was.

And maybe, for a minute, I forgot it was all pretend.

Chapter 9

Kiara

Heartworm

noun

1. a relationship or friendship you can't get out of your
    head

.   .   .

"Let's go, we have a plane to catch." I get very impatient at airports. I'm like a brown Dad. I always want to be there several hours earlier, I have to check the passports and boarding cards on a half-an-hourly basis and I tend to lose my glasses to the top of my head more often than not.

Kabir was jogging behind me with the bags, struggling to catch up under the additional weight, "I'm coming, I'm coming. God, you're even more incessant at the airport. I didn't think it was possible."

I smiled, "I'm full of surprises."

"Besides, it's not like the plane is going to leave without you. It's *your* plane."

I laughed, "Right. Sorry, I just get very hyper at airports."

He rolled his eyes, keeping his voice completely flat, "Really? I hadn't noticed."

.   .   .

We settled into the jet and I couldn't help the excitement that was bubbling through my veins. I must've been bouncing in my seat because Kabir said, "Calm down love. You're behaving like you've had ten cups of coffee. Remind me to get you a decaf next time."

I glared at him, "You think you're so funny, don't you? God, I can't stand you."

He relaxed into his seat, shooting me a lazy, lopsided smirk, "I know, love."

"I have a dress fitting before the dinner tomorrow at headquarters." I love the term headquarters. It always made me feel like I was living out my fantasies of being a professional spy—other than the part where I work a regular nine-to-five for a multi-billion Dollar corporation, that is. Every year, Shah Enterprises organizes a banquet dinner at the London headquarters to celebrate the year.

"I have my tux fitting at the same time." My heart raced at the thought of Kabir in a tuxedo.

I felt curiosity gnawing at me as I asked my next question, "How much longer do you think we'll need to keep all this up for?"

His face went blank and he looked whiter than a ghost, "Depends. I—Uh—I think I'm going to take a nap. Wake me up in a couple hours."

I nodded, unable to say anything. I felt my gut sink slightly with the way he completely avoided my question. I couldn't help but wonder if it was because of the shift in our dynamic. It was slowly beginning to become clear that neither of us truly hated each other.

Maybe I'm wrong.

.　　.　　.

Kabir

Forelsket

noun

1. the intense, almost unreal feeling that comes with the beginning of love; when you start to fall in love

.   .   .

I didn't sleep a wink on the entire flight. I closed my eyes but all I could think about was her. About the mistake I was making by remaining quiet. I leaned my head on her arm while I pretended to sleep, needing to be near her.

.   .   .

"I just got a text from my assistant. Turns out our fittings are at the same place. Works out perfectly actually," she was pretty chirpy for the first thing in the morning. Different to how she usually was at work. We'd already grabbed coffee at her favourite coffee shop—which I agreed was pretty damn good and we were heading to our fitting.

"Why exactly is that?"

"I get to see your tux before dinner tonight, and you get to see my dress." She mumbled the last part but I could make out just enough. I smiled at my fake girlfriend as she sipped on her coffee, tendrils of steam wafting around her lips. We got to the boutique and were immediately whisked away to separate dressing rooms. I'd gone with a classic black and white tuxedo, so that I could match whatever colour she wore.

Kabir, you're killing me here. Matching outfits? You're a goner.

I changed and sat down to wait for her to finish. We were on opposite sides of a large room with red velvet flooring. There were two big mirrors with pedestals in front of each, next to which stood two large dressing rooms, one on either side. Both closed with matching red velvet curtains as well. The entire boutique reminded me of something straight out of the Shakespearean era. I scoured the entire room with my eyes while I waited, taking in the chandeliers and tapestries. Then, she walked out. And I think my heart stopped beating.

I thought maybe I'd forgotten how to breathe.

Or maybe I was learning how to.

She was standing on top of the pedestal in front of the mirror closest to her dressing room, "Kabir?"

I think she must've called my names a few times because, "Kabir? Kabir? Hello? Are you okay?"

I stood up suddenly, "I—Um—Fine. I'm fine."

She went back to her reflection. Her hair was tied up in a messy bun with loose strands framing the edges of her face, "What do you think?"

I tried to come up with a reasonable answer. Something that would actually suffice everything I wanted to express. "I can't breathe."

She turned around quickly and rushed toward me, touching my forehead and cheeks with the back of her hand like she was checking me for a fever, "Kabir, are you sure you're okay? You're worrying me."

I pressed her hand on my cheek with my palm, losing myself in her auburn eyes, "You make it hard to breathe."

Her cheeks went red again and she retreated her hand. I could see the remnants of a smile flit across her mouth as she said, "Stop making me worried like that."

"Careful, you're behaving like you actually care about me."

She rolled her eyes, ignoring the smile on my face.

She didn't deny it.

"So, do you like it?" she whispered.

I turned to one side to hide the grin on my face, "Eh, it'll do. I guess" She slapped me across the arm, laughing.

I twirled her, "Yes. I think I just might like it."

·   ·   ·

I was waiting for her outside the car, leaning against the doorframe in the freezing cold. Jeeves was driving us to the event. He came and waited next to me,

"Good evening to you Sir."

"Good evening Jeeves. How're you doing?"

"Very well Sir," he smiled, his wrinkled cheeks touching his worn eyes. Jeeves was old, but Kiara had said that he'd weathered life with her. He took a breath of the crisp wind and started, "Sir, if I may?" he hesitated, waiting for me to give him the green light to speak his mind.

"Please, by all means."

"Miss Kiara is young, and perhaps ambitious beyond her means. But that young girl in there has so much love to give. Maybe she needs a reminder that we can fall in love many times throughout life. Just because you get hurt once doesn't mean that you never try again. Love is a beautiful thing, I think she needs someone to show her that again."

He winked at me and jogged back over to the driver's seat as Kiara walked outside. I thought about his words for a moment. *Is he telling me what I think he's telling me? Is it obvious that I'm in love?*

I pushed those thoughts to the back of my mind and focused on Kiara. I didn't think it was possible for her to get any more beautiful than she was, but somehow, she did. Her golden gown hugged her skin in all the right places and I could hardly take my eyes off her.

She pushed my jaw up to meet my mouth, "You're staring, *love*."

I frowned at her, opening the car door, "Don't steal my line." She just smiled and entered the car, shaking her head gently at me.

•   •   •

It wasn't long before we arrived at company headquarters—as Kiara likes to call it. I'd been there a few times many years ago but the building is like no other. It rivals some of the buildings in Dubai. She sighed as we stepped out of the car, staring wistfully at the building, "HQ."

"It's beautiful."

She smiled, "Dad did a great job. Which reminds me, you're meeting Mum and Dad for the first time tonight."

I held out my arm for her and she grabbed it. We began walking inside as she gave me instructions on the whole meeting the parents thing.

"All you have to do is remain calm. My Dad loves you anyway, he'd never trust you with the Dubai office if he didn't."

I chuckled, "He might not love me so much when he sees my hands on his daughter."

She straightened, not giving herself enough time to blush, "That's another thing, no being touchy. I'll be touchy enough for the both of us. You can hug me, but I'd assume my strict Indian Dad doesn't love the idea of a man having his hands around my waist."

I groaned.

She wrapped her hands around my waist, staring into my eyes jokingly, "Do you miss having your hands around me that much Kabir Kapoor?"

I wrapped my hands around her waist tightly in response, "Maybe." She recoiled under my touch, pink tinting her cheeks. We exited the lift and entered the banquet hall.

"We're here. Don't leave my side."

I smiled, "Never."

And maybe I meant it.

She spent the next hour introducing me to fifty different men. They were all relatively the same: wealthy and balding if not already bald. It was nice to meet all the people she'd grown up around though. They all seemed really proud to have her as their CFO.

.　　.　　.

Kiara

"I think Pintu Uncle was my favorite."

I laughed, "Pintu Uncle is definitely one of the more chill ones," I could see Pinky Auntie in my peripheral vision and I swear I had a heart attack, "10 o'clock, Pinky Auntie. Abort. Abort."

Kabir held me firmly, "We're going to have to talk to her at some point, love. Why don't you let me lead negotiations?"

I groaned and followed him as he approached Pinky Auntie. She'd spotted us and was bouncing over in her kitten heels. They made that incessant clicking sound as she sashayed in our direction.

"Pinky Auntie," I barely managed to grit out my words, "So—*good*, to see you." Kabir elbowed me slightly as I stalled on my words.

He kissed her hand, "Lovely to see you, Pinky Auntie." She blushed and fanned her face, turning a petunia pink. I tried not to laugh.

"Such a gentleman," She giggled sheepishly in that Pinky Auntie way of hers.

He just bowed and smiled, taking his place next to me. Pinky Auntie bored us with stories about how she's trying to find a suitable husband for her daughter Dimple and made good mention of what an incredible second catch Kabir is.

He is a pretty great catch.

I kept getting stuck on the words 'second catch'. I'd forgotten that Jai was even a part of my life. It still aches sometimes. Thinking about it all. But it feels like a closing wound. Something that I have to clean up a couple more times, and it'll be good as new. Like it never happened.

It sucks to think about it that way. Especially after everything we'd been through together. But I have to move on.

I looked back at Kabir, who was still politely entertaining Pinky Auntie, and I couldn't help but feel relief. Pure unadulterated relief.

I don't think moving on is as bad as it sounds.

·   ·   ·

Kabir

"Mr. Shah! So good to see you." Mr. Shah looked exactly as I'd seen him last. He hadn't aged a day. But I guess that's how he always looked. Hair just slightly graying, suit always clean and sharp and always grinning. His grin reminds me of a Cheshire cat. So unknowingly intelligent.

He hugged me, "Kabir! Good to see you, Son." He calls everyone 'Son'. He hugged Kiara and we all retreated to a corner of the room to talk. Mrs. Shah joined us, giving both of us brief hugs before excusing herself to mingle with the other guests. She assured me, "I'll be back to catch up with you Kabir," and then winked.

"Dad, we have something to tell you."

He frowned, "Is something wrong with the office? Tell me and I'll get whoever I need to get on the phone." He gestured to his phone and started typing in numbers vigorously.

Kiara fastened her hand around my callused fingers. She sunk her fingers around mine and gripped tightly. I curved my hand around hers, gripping her small fingers with my own.

She chuckled lightly before beginning but I could tell it was a nervous laugh, "No, Dad." She held our intertwined hands up, "We're—dating."

He paused, no smile to be seen anywhere near his face, "Oh." He looked puzzled, like he was doing a cost-benefit analysis in his head.

He kept his face and tone extremely serious as he asked, "Is he treating you well?"

She squeezed my hand, "The best."

"Does he give you enough freedom?"

"More than enough."

He turned to me, "Do you care about her?"

"More than anything."

He started smiling that knowing smile of his again, "Congratulations!" He pulled his daughter away from me to give her a hug.

He turned to hug me and whispered in my ear, "You hurt her, and I kill you." He smiled as he pulled away, whispering one more thing, "I know you won't though. I know that look. It's the same look I had when I married her Mother."

.   .   .

Kiara

It felt like forever before we finally sat down for the actual meal. All I had to do now was survive the toasts, and then I could actually enjoy my night. This dinner usually goes from relatively tame to completely wild once the clock hits midnight. It's like pulling a reverse Cinderella.

My Dad stood to give his usual toast.

Tink. Tink. Tink.

"Thank you all so much for being here. This year has been one of the most incredible ones for us. We appointed a new CFO and CEO, opened an office in Dubai and managed to triple our profits from last year."

Applause sounded through the room.

"I would like to sincerely thank all of you for working so diligently this year to make it our best so far. I am excited to present to you our very own Kabir Kapoor, who is heading up our brand new Dubai office." Kabir stood up and gave everyone a small wave before sitting back down. I tried to ignore the booming of my heart in my chest as he winked at me.

What happened to hating him?

"I am also excited to announce that our CFO will be returning to London headquarters after successfully getting our Dubai office up and running."

Kabir turned toward me with pure devastation on his face. He looked like I'd just slapped him. I couldn't hear anything but the ringing in my ears as he got up from the table and left the room. I felt like I couldn't breathe. I thought for a minute that my heart had stopped working. I stared at Dhruv in a silent plea for help. He gave me a look from across the table, mouthing "Go." He smiled in that big brother way of his, and somehow it made everything that much easier.

I could tell everyone was watching us. Watching this. But somehow, I didn't care. I went after him, searching through endless hallways for my fake boyfriend. I took off my heels and started running in his direction, "Kabir! Stop!"

He turned around and I could see tears in his eyes.

"What's wrong with you?" I felt breathless—partly from the running and partly from the way he was looking at me.

"Why didn't you tell me you were going back?" His voice was cool and calculated, the mask right back up where it belonged. Except, it didn't belong there. Especially not for me. Especially not after I'd spent so long thawing it out. Especially not now that I knew the real Kabir.

"It's not like it was ever a—uh—a secret. The Dubai office got set up a little faster than I initially thought, so I— I decided to prepone my return to London. Staying in Dubai was never uh—permanent anyways." I choked on my words, my throat willing itself further closed as I ended each sentence. My own heart broke at the thought of leaving Dubai. I loved London, but somehow, I loved Dubai more. It felt like home. It felt like the place that healed me. Healed a broken heart; a broken person. A person I'd forgotten existed.

And if I was being honest with myself, I wasn't ready to leave. But there was nothing for me to stay for.

Unless there is.

"Why didn't you tell me? What happened to sixty days?" He was whispering now, like speaking any louder would make all of this too real. Too painful.

"Why does it even matter?" I felt myself getting angry, and upset, and heartbroken. Quickly. A single tear raced down my cheek.

"Because it does matter, Kiara. It matters to *me*. Stay. Just stay." The light in his eyes was dimmed and pleading, like he was begging for me to agree. I wanted to break down in tears at the sight of him. Of his face with that look. The look of a broken person. The look that *I'd* given him.

"That's not a reason, Kabir. Give me one good reason why I should stay," I whispered into the distance between us.

"Because I'm bloody in love with you Kiara. And I hate it. I don't know how to make it stop. We're supposed to hate each other. Hell, I'm pretty sure you still hate me."

Another tear slipped down my cheek as I whispered, "No, I don't."

"I don't know how to love people. They call me a heartless monster because I only know how to hurt and push away. But I can't stop loving you. No matter how hard I try. No matter how much I convince myself that this is a bad idea. That I'm bad for you. No matter how much I convince myself that I don't need you. None of it works. Nothing works, because it physically hurts to be away from you. I tried my hardest not to feel anything. Not to feel the flames that sound through my blood when you touch me. Not to feel the cracking in my chest when you smile. Not to feel my knees buckle when you give me a small salute in the kitchen. I can't go anywhere without thinking about you. Not work, not *my own bed*. Nowhere." He laughed and it was almost bitter. Like he had convinced himself he was completely alone. That he'd lost. "I didn't know what the word meant until we met. I thought love was supposed to be easy. But it's the hardest thing I've ever done. Because it isn't supposed to be easy. It's supposed to hurt. It's supposed to hurt and still—still be worth it all at the end. So please, just stay." He was breathless by the end. Then, in three strides, he closed the few feet between us.

And kissed me.

Chapter 10

Kiara

Kintsugi. I think that's what everyone's searching for in their lives. The gold that'll bind their broken pieces together. Make them whole again. Stronger.

I like the way Kabir put it. Love isn't easy. And it isn't supposed to be. It's supposed to suck. But the whole point is that it's supposed to suck and still be worth it all at the end.

I think I found mine. And it just so happens to be my grumpy colleague in the city of my dreams.